S0-ARK-596

1001 ARCHITECTURAL EXPRESSIONS OF PSYCHE, SOUL, & SPIRIT

FRANK AZZOPARDI

Copyright © 2012, Frank Azzopardi

ISBN: 978-0-9860253-0-3

Library of Congress Control Number: 2012917413

All Rights Reserved. No part of this book may be reproduced or transmitted in any form or by any means, electronic or mechanical, including photo-copying, recording, or by any information storage and retrieval system, with-out written permission from the author, except for the inclusion of brief quotations in a review.

Printed in the United States of America.

ACKNOWLEDGMENTS

To my dear parents, Charlie and Jane, who by their courage and strength, wisdom and insight, have proven to be quality pillars of stamina and integrity; I thank you for your encouragement.

To my dear brother Mario, who has always been there for me with good judgment and common sense solutions; I thank you for helping me to stay focused and on track from start to finish.

And finally I wish to thank my dear nieces, Stephanie, Amy, and Ellie, whose eager spirits and enthusiastic love of life have powered me with an abundance of bright and clear energy and eagerness.

At this time I also wish to thank Maureen from FirstEditing.com., a Florida-based editorial service, for her encouragement and professionalism in helping make this book happen. Many thanks to the staff at Bookmasters of Ohio as well for their Nobel professionalism in helping to make this book a work of art in and of itself.

One way or another each one of you have contributed to generating in me a novel sense of inspiration and creativity, empowering my own Psyche, Soul, and Spirit, with the ability to touch the Psyche, Soul, and Spirit, of the inanimate. For without this spirit touch, this bridge between contemporary architecture and a new era of expressive architecture could not have been built. A bridge which has provided today's architectural community with the means to redefine architecture as we know it.

About the Author

I was born on the upper east side of Manhattan and raised in New York City, surroundings that allowed me to develop a sense of creative individuality and led me into a life dedicated to art and design. I earned a BFA in fine arts from the Parsons School of Design and painted scores of residential murals throughout New York City following graduation. Feeling client input was cramping my style, I went underground and started working with different forms of personal expression. My creative persona along with my artistic lifestyle in one of the most diverse and vibrant cities in the world allowed me to view basic architectural forms in a new light. The influence of my urban surroundings on the artist in me spurred me into creating thousands of pen and ink drawings of architectural expressions. This book includes the 1,001 most diverse.

IMAGINATION ALLOWS YOU TO SEE THE WORLD IN A DIFFERENT WAY.

INTRODUCTION

The human persona is made up of a community of elements which cannot be heard from. They are embedded deep in our being and cannot be explained in terms of the physio-mechanical or the neuro-chemical. They are intangibles in our dimension, invisibles in their dimension. Ghosts deep in a unidentifiable dimension of the mind. Yet, for all their elusiveness, the intrinsic value of these elements to our being is immeasurable. For these elements form the cornerstone of our being, our inner-self.

Composed of Psyche, Soul, and Spirit, the inner-self strives to make itself known to the Brain, Heart, and Blood of one's consciousness, the outer-self. This interaction of inner-self and outer-self takes place in the deepest, most secluded chambers of the mind, the town hall of one's being. Here, all the elements, both seen and unseen, of one's self enter open discussion, formulating and solidifying a complicated web of principles, concepts, values, concerns, attitudes, and passions that make up one's personality. This hidden chamber is at a halfway point, mid dimension, between inner-self (Psyche, Soul, and Spirit) and outer-self (Brain, Heart, and Blood). The dialogue exchanged in these open discussions provides both entities the means of communicating and exchanging views, ideas, interests, and wants that are necessary to allow the inner-self to make itself known by way of outwardly expressed deeds and actions. Unfortunately, expression of the inner-self's wants and needs is not as easy as it may sound. There are many times when one's inner-self cannot concretely state its position. Times when it cannot sufficiently energize itself to the point that the inner-self's manifestations can stand up proud and boisterously enough to satisfactorily convince other members of the town hall of the inner-self's convictions. Hence, the transferring of the inner-self to the outer-self is now bogged down in a quagmire of town hall bickering and quarreling over differences of opinions and concepts. The circumstances that have entrapped the inner-self in an arena of prolonged debate now lead the entire community of town hall elements into a highly charged emotional state of mental anguish and conflict. Mental trickery and deceit begin to wear out the inner spirit and weaken the outer-self's heart. As a result of such mental deception, successful expression of the inner-self to the outer-self becomes sabotaged to the point that it is snuffed out completely. The inner-self thereby is sentenced to an imprisoned existence where gloom and despondency prevail. The inner-self's failure to successfully communicate its needs of expression to the consciousness imprisons the Soul, Psyche, and Spirit to a dimension of misery and unhappiness, incubating hidden internal turmoil, confusion, and restlessness. This negativity and restlessness will not find calm until it is rescued by the saving grace of the light. The light here is any one of a number of externals absorbed by the conscious and introduced into the town hall. Once the inner recognizes the appropriate external as the solution to its inadequacy, the inner spirit and the external heart will once again strengthen. This strengthening of spirit and heart will empower the soul and psyche with more than enough positive energy to deliver it from the quagmire of prolonged bickering and quarreling in the town hall.

Those individuals who are fortunate enough to be artists, writers, or musicians have found the externals necessary to release inner expressions and relieve anxieties generated by tensions in the town hall. For those individuals who are less fortunate, I offer the contents of this book and the light of its message as a means of providing their inner-self a suitable mouthpiece for communicating with their outer-self, their consciousness, and the world in which all beings live, work, and play in. The contents of this book offer light in the form of 1001 external expressions of architecture capable of extracting the imprisoned inner-self out of its hostile predicament. It is absolutely imperative that the light be external in origin. For it is with the external world, humanity as a whole, that one's inner being seeks communication with and gratification from. I can think of no other worldly light that offers greater liberation of one's Psyche, Soul, and Spirit than that which is offered by Expressive Architecture. Expressive Architecture provides the human soul with the means to express visually that which cannot be expressed verbally. As a result of the saving grace offered by the light of these architectural expressions, what could not be said verbally can now be said visually.

The eyes are the threshold from the external world to the inner. A pathway to the soul. What the eyes see, the soul feels. When one's heart feels that its eyes have seen the architectural expression that best represents its soul, all community elements of the town hall get emotionally charged with positivity and enthusiasm over the prospect of being portrayed accurately and aesthetically in and to the physical external world. The responsibility of deciding whether or not one should embark on the emotionally charged endeavor of building a physical world's expressive structure lies with the external of ones being, the Brain, the Heart, and the Blood. The conscious. This personal decision should be driven by a passion to openly express one's self veraciously to the world and not be based on rational or other pragmatic considerations. The persona that elects to erect is one who knows itself and achieves inner rewards of delightment, accomplishment, and satisfaction over successfully erecting and living in a structure expressive of its personality. Additional gratification is derived over successfully allowing its friends, neighbors, and other members of its physical world to get a sense of who and what this individual persona is about.

Once the inner Psyche, Soul, and Spirit successfully express themselves architecturally, they have said what they needed to say in the form of a 3D extension of one's inner-self. A 3D expression that has pronounced the inner-self physically in everyday life. It has made its presence known, as well as allowing its spirit to find itself in the community. A balance is achieved between what needs to be expressed outwardly versus what needs to be felt inwardly. As a result of this architectural expression and the harmonious balance it has created, a healthy union of inner-self, consciousness, the external community, and humanity comes into being. A union providing a renewed sense of wholeness and purposefulness. This renewed sense of self-worth now means that the town hall bickering and the negativity generated over the issue of how to best express itself openly will come to a end. The reaching of an agreement on soul opening now means that peace and serenity will once again fill the town hall, putting an end to the mental anguish and anxiety it created. The inner turmoil and restlessness of the inner-self will be replaced with positive energy and tranquility, providing one's persona the freedom and space it needs to pursue whatever adventurous and entertaining interests it may wish to engage in. The inner has been liberated. The battle is over.

1

INANIMATE SOULS

Neutrons are said to possess a neutral or no electrical charge, while protons are said to possess a positive electrical charge. These two units form the nucleus of an atom and are held together by negatively charged electrons revolving around the nucleus. This nucleus is the Soul of the atom. Since the universe is made up of atoms, anything and everything, both animate and inanimate, seen and unseen, that either emits or absorbs energy has a Soul. A Soul which not only motivates and influences, but also inspires and encourages its surroundings by way of its internal source of power.

With inanimate Soul comes Psyche. Not as powerful in transmitting electrical impulses as the human Psyche, but powerful enough to generate inspiration and motivation to everything within the realm of its influence. Electrical impulses, psychic vibes that allow the inner energies of one inanimate object to connect with other inner energies emitted by other Psyches, both near and far.

The sensitivities of the Soul and Psyche delicately refine the absorption of external energies into emotional idealisms and sentimentalities that give the Soul and Psyche Spirit.

The idea that the inanimate have no Soul or Psyche because they lack qualities associated with living organisms, such as verbal communication or motor abilities, is that of the shallow-minded. The inanimate that I am referring to here is that of the architectural structure expressive of a person's Psyche, Soul, and Spirit. An architectural expression, which not only emits its own personal energy while absorbing energy emitted by its inhabitant, but also the energies and passions that it absorbed from its creators during its conception and through its construction. Energies that not only affect the usage of this architectural structure for as long as it lives, but will also enable the structure to endure, thrive, persevere and continue evolving long after its creators are gone.

The inanimate soul of a architectural expression is of importance to us because of its role in the symbiotic relationship it enters with the inhabitant of the architectural expression. This close association of Psyche, Soul, and Spirit of different dimensions, occupying the same space and time, entangle both entities into a companionship that is mutually beneficial. Occupation of the architectural expression by the inhabitant has now forced the architectural expression into a state of a meaningfulness and purposefulness. Not only is the inhabitant appreciated by the architectural expression, but is now desperately needed to give the architectural expression drive and justification for its existence. The architectural expression's primary purpose, that of providing one's inner-self the means to express itself openly, as well as the utilitarian worth of the architectural expression, has given the Psyche, Soul, and Spirit of the architectural expression life. Its birth has given the architectural expression its own sense of self-worth and personal individualism. Its heartbeat is energized by the satisfaction it receives from knowing that it speaks for all elements of the inhabitant's innerself when it expresses visually that which cannot be expressed verbally. Its breath is in its purpose of serving as the mouthpiece for the town hall; it does not breath or exhale air, it breathes and exhales purpose. In exchange for its purpose, life, and love it receives, the architectural expression releases its own positive vibes and energy, providing the inhabitant with a renewed enthusiasm for life, a renewed love for work, and a renewed sense of gratitude and satisfaction for play.

This release of vibes and energies by the architectural expressions Psyche, Soul, and Spirit are intangible essentials of all existence that is tangible.

The Brain, the Heart, and the Blood are tangibles here and now. The Psyche, the Soul, and the Spirit are intangibles also here and now. They remain when the physical Brain, Heart, and Blood no longer exist. Of the Brain the Psyche remains, of the Heart the Soul remains, and of the Blood the Spirit remains. The traveling of the Blood is the traveling of the Spirit. As the Blood travels from Heart to Brain, the Spirit will travel from Soul to Psyche. The Brain hosts the Psyche, the Heart hosts the Soul, and the Blood hosts the Spirit. Just as the energy of the Psyche, Soul, and Spirit existed long before the Brain, Heart, and Blood came to be, so too will the Psyche, Soul, and Spirit remain as unseen energy long after the Brain, Heart, and Blood perish.

The Psyche, Soul, and Spirit make up the inner-self and lie deep in the organs that house them. They are locked in another dimension and therefore are hard to communicate with. In the up-over dimension, there is the outer-self made up of Brain, Heart, and Blood. In a second dimension, the down-under dimension, there lies an inner-self made up of Psyche, Soul, and Spirit. Both dimensions of self occupy the same space and time. The union of the up-over dimension with the down-under dimension is life. From the traveling of the Soul in the Heart to the Psyche in the Brain by way of the Spirit in the Blood arises the need for the personal expression of the energy behind the life of the individual persona. The energy behind the life and the being of the persona is the energy of one's inner-self. The essence of one's being, the true blue behind the scenes, the character and personality of the persona. Trapped deep in another unreachable dimension, the down-under inner-self cannot easily express itself verbally like its counterpart, the up-over outer-self. So it must express itself visually. Each and every visual expression of the unreachable inner-self is worth a thousand words by the outer-self.

The five senses, those of sight, hearing, touch, taste, and smell, flavor the Psyche by introducing outside variables to the Brain. Here we are concerned with the sense of sight for two reasons. First, it is the sense of sight that introduces these drawings as external variables to the Brain for presentation to the inner-self so it can consider which one of these drawings is best suited to release, as well as outwardly express inner issues and energies in the same dimension as it counterpart, the up-over outer-self. And secondly, once the inner-self has expressed itself outwardly, in the same dimension as its counterpart, it is the sense of sight that will deliver final gratification to the hidden inner-self once that inner-self views itself in 3D.

Once introduced to the mental theater of the Brain, the drawings presented here dance with one unseen element of the inner-self after another until the inner-self finds a compatible dance partner. That dance partner being an architectural drawing that is a visual reflection of its attitude, beliefs, convictions, and passions. At this time a persona's deepest internal components of Psyche, Soul, and Spirit begin to incubate into what was, up until now, nothing more than a 3D fantasy.

2

CULTURAL ARCHITECTURE

The great pharaohs of ancient Egypt directed the architects of that era to build grandiose temples and tombs that followed prescribed rules and procedures as well as mathematical principles of algebra and geometry. These grandiose structures visually reflect the social order of government, religion, technical, and cultural skills of various elements of that society. Not only does the greatness of these pharaohs and their society live on through the permanence of these durable, amazing architectural wonders, but so too does their fundamental belief of existence beyond death.

The metropolitan shrines of Europe, more commonly known as cathedrals, reflect the devotion of the Christian society of the era in which they were built. Their impressive ornamentation, which adorns both the outside of these massive structures and the inside of the large chambers of congregation that they house, gives us a sense of the devotion and pious respect given by the communities that those cathedrals serve. The cultural servitude given to those communities, and the respect given back to these structures by those communities, has led not only to their longevity and endurance, but also to that of the religio-politico movement of the society that created them.

The Aztecs built pyramids, enormous in size, that elevated sacrificial altars high into the sky. Take one look at these super-sized structures and it's not hard to tell that their purpose was to offer sacrifices to the gods. Their towering strength and brutality offer testimony to the bloody sacrifices that took place atop those pyramids. The plazas that surround these Goliath structures give us an idea of just how great ceremonial activities must have been and the value that was placed on those activities.

The tall corporate city skyscrapers of wealthy America bear mention here as well. They represent the value placed on them by our thriving capitalistic society. They are a visual testimony to the huge amounts of capital raised by corporations in today's stock market. Economic considerations of construction costs are dwarfed in comparison to the primary purpose of these super-structures, whose purpose is to convey the corporations' image of being competitively safe and secure, snug amongst their competitors.

All four architectural examples mentioned reflect the cultural values, psychological attitudes, and inner-selves of the societies responsible for their erection. Each individual persona of those societies is cumulatively expressed by the architectural structures they built.

And so it stands to reason that as we now enter yet another era of humanity, we need new architecture that is more a reflection of who we are today: a society striving for betterment while at the same time not conforming to any sacred principle. A free-spirited people. Each striving for individuality and perfectionism while at the same time defying all logical considerations. We outwardly, and shamelessly, disregard all valid reasoning and seem to pride ourselves on our irrational behavior, while at the same time adhering to underlying values and principles respected only by the individual's inner-self. Pragmatism appears to have been put on the back burner for the long haul into an uncertain future. Important decisions that affect matters of our daily living seem to be made recklessly and awkwardly in regards to their desired outcome.

Our disrespect for all that is rational, coupled by our daredevilish reasoning, has led to the type of irrational behavior that can best be described, in a general sense, as bizarre. Combine this bizarre behavior of today's people with the awakening of the individual's need and desire to successfully express his or hers inner-self's deepest passions and you have crossed over a bridge into a new era ripe for joyfully fulfilling and gratifying architecture. A time of architectural renaissance in which there are no parameters or boundaries to limit structural expression of Psyche, Soul, and Spirit. A time in which there are no fixed templates of consciousness to restrict creative expression of individuality. Joyfully expressive structures that become outer extensions of our inner-selves. Such outer extensions say visually of our inner-selves what can't be expressed verbally. An outer extension, such as a differently designed architectural structure, becomes a sort of badge of our soul, our inner identity, our deepest inner-selves. Every inner-self is different and requires its own personal factors of satisfaction. One's self-designed architectural structure reflects one's inner-self by projecting the energy of that personality's inner-self onto the design project.

Hence emerges the purposefulness and usefulness of this book and the drawings of architectural expressions contained therein.

This book's aim is to take the minds of today's architectural community to places they would not go without the aid of these drawings. Places where architecture is no longer about the individual, but about what's in the individual. It should stimulate thought, as well as discussion, that will begin to transform our cultural beliefs and values into visual experiences that reflect contemporary life. Visual experiences that give dimension to personal, social, physical, and psychological elements of everyday life in today's society.

Experiences that architecturally conceptualize the Psyche, Soul, and Spirit of the individual as they and that individual relate to, as well as fit into, their place in society.

Architecturalization that becomes psychological expression, as well as architectural representation and visual extensions, of the individual's inner-self.

Architectural expressions that satisfy the creativity of the inner-self. Expressions that not only speak for themselves as great engineering feats, but also delight another segment of our Psyche, Soul, and Spirit; that of pride in our amazingly personalized reflection of our individuality.

Architectural expressions that in and of themselves say we are ingenious builders. That not only do we build as great builders, but as artisans striving for betterment and cultural awareness of what we are capable of accomplishing as a people living and working together as individuals, each with his or her own personal sense and pride of self.

3

HOW IT WORKS

In this chapter I will introduce 10 release mechanisms that are designed to help the outer-self play a role in freeing its trapped counterpart, the inner-self. I have termed these release mechanisms "Personifiers." Personifiers unlock and then transform trapped inner issues of the Psyche, passions of the Soul, and convictions of the Spirit into physical 3D personalities by modifying and/or converting these geometric drawings into authentic representation of one's inner-self. The relationship of these Personifiers to the inner issues they free are, for the most part, known only to the underlying hidden inner-self responsible for their release. An inner that is a culmination of one's life experiences and energies directed into the respective segments of the issues, passions, and convictions that are of value to that persona's inner-self. Experiences that have made a permanent imprint, a defining mark, on one's up-over outer-self, as well as one's down-under inner-self. Such imprints or marks become trademarks of attitude, of one specific individual, and therefore cannot be adopted or incorporated into another persona's inventory of issues, passions, or convictions that make up one's hidden inner. There are no fixed templates or carbon copies of inner-selves that one can slip into to accurately portray his or her inner-self. Since there is no duplication of inner-self, it becomes necessary for one's persona to independently convert these architectural drawings into expressions that reflect the individual and not the social, religious, or political issues of his surrounding environment. The soon-to-be inhabitant should not be as interested in the completed architectural structure being an object of architecture, but as something that fulfills the deepest dimension of one's interior when nothing else does. Something that cultivates emotional well-being and internal happiness, something that allows the inhabitant to feel calmer and more content with life in general. Something that will allow the inhabitant to live happier, naturally and effectively.

Unlike psychiatry, this process of selecting a compatible expression is not one by which a individual's persona is studied or diagnosed through some form of psycho architectural analyzation. Rather, it is that portion of the individual's persona that studies the Psyche, Soul, and Spirit of the 1001 architectural expressions, searching for an external physical counterpart possessing the perfect architectural frame of being in which both the Psyche, Soul, and Spirit of the animate persona and the Psyche, Soul, and Spirit of the inanimate architectural expression can sustain a long lasting, harmonious symbiotic existence. This search for a compatible counterpart is not accomplished by externals looking in. It is accomplished by the internal inner-self, that which lies hidden in the shadows of another dimension, looking out.

Figure A is our sample architectural expression that will be used to illustrate the effects that come about through the application of each of the 10 Personifiers.

Figure A

When one release mechanism is used, it plays the role of a Personifier; when multiple release mechanisms are used, their roles are that of Modifiers. The last conversion by the last Modifier is the Personifier. Our sample architectural expression in Figure A has all the attributes necessary to take part in a harmonious symbiotic relationship between dweller and structure. It, along with all the other expressions in this book, is capable of representing as well as satisfying an immense number of inner-selves without their geometric composition being altered. When the deepest segments of one's inner-self, that which is too deep to have itself heard, are successfully represented, and that inner feels it has been born in 3D, the process of applying modifiers stops. In short, the final modification has personified the original expression into a 3D representation that gives the glory and greatness to the unheard of inner-self that it strives so hard to achieve.

The Cube came into power as the supreme answer to all architectural projects by way of its pragmatic utilitarian worth. It was never meant to be a means of free-spirited expression, hence it stands to reason that in today's era of heightened spiritual awareness of one's inner-self and the need for that self to successfully express itself as an individual, the Cube has become obsolete. Usage of the Cube today reflects personas that are mundane in their existence, personas that are conservative in their living. Not because of any ideological beliefs, but for fear of rocking the boat by stepping out of the box. These personas are passive and easily led, weak and easily influenced. The inanimate characteristics of the Cube, its Psyche, Soul, and Spirit, are not much different than that of the inhabitant selecting this form of habitat, and therefore supportive of the negative issues of that blend of human companionship. The neat and orderly conservative arrangement of parallel edges and perfectly square corners say that the structure's being is snug in its correctness. Just like its human inhabitant, this structure is mundane in its existence. It contributes no uplifting or creative energy to the symbiotic relationship between the dweller and the dwelling. The negativity emitted by the inner being of the Cube, coupled with the conservative restrained deprivation of inner expression on the part of the inhabitant, leads to an environment in which negativity becomes trapped by all six planes of the Cube. Lacking an adequate means of release or creative outlet of inner expression, trapped negativity is left with no other alternative but to keep bouncing off of all six planes, generating a squirrelly energy field for its inhabitants to occupy.

Whereas Cubistic energy bounces back and forth, Spherical energy rotates harmoniously and evenly in one direction, much like that of the Earth rotating on its axis. Cubistic energy is like that of a rat trapped in a wooden box, attempting to escape by gnawing and scratching at the inner walls of the box. Spherical energy swims like an angel fish in a glass bowl. Its naturally balanced utopian form and structurally mesmerizing proportions allow it to generate feelings of absolute tranquility. It is as beautiful and as perfect as Mother Nature herself. Its magnetic visual ability to adventurously attract the dreamy, the heavenly, and the pleasantly abstract allow it to take on the role of architecturally representing personality traits associated with the romantic, the glamorous, the bedazzled and the spellbound, the magical and the enchanted.

Although the structural elements of the pyramid are more reflective of nature's tranquility than that of the Cube, they are no match for the aura of peacefulness reflected by the Sphere. Both Sphere and Pyramid provide an environment that allows the inhabitant to absorb their internal energies of peace and serenity as those energies constantly flow harmoniously and uninterrupted. This same flow also allows for the structure to absorb internal energies from the inhabitant as both the structure and the inhabitant are emitting, absorbing, exchanging, and sharing internal energies. In the Cube, energy transmission is interrupted every time that energy bounces off of a wall. As a result, its absorption by the inhabitant is also interrupted and therefore not as harmonious as it would be in a Spherical or Pyramidical environment. In most circumstances, the concentration of Cubistic energy and Spherical energy remain evenly dispersed throughout the structure. This is not so with the Pyramid; energy at the base of the Pyramid is not as focused or as concentrated as energy at the Pyramid's peak, where all four triangular sides converge on one common point. Structural energies of the Pyramid are constantly being generated at this common point, directly opposite and farthest away from its base. This generation creates an accumulation of excessive energy, with only one way to travel in order for it to disseminate, and that is away from the common vertex to the base.

The scope of happiness in the symbiotic relationship of inhabitant and structure widens when they both share the same passions and convictions. The flowing of Pyramidical Energies to the base, when the base is on the bottom, are energy dynamics that would be best appreciated by inhabitants possessing personality traits associated with the self-centered, the secretive, and the selfish. Pyramids, or Triangles, in this position release energies and issues of the inner-self concerning the mystical, the mathematical, the pessimistic, and the introverted.

The flowing of Pyramidical Energies to the base, when the base is on top, are energy dynamics that would be best appreciated by inhabitants possessing personality traits associated with the outgoing, the friendly, and the trustworthy. Pyramids, or Triangles, in this position release energies and issues of the inner-self concerning the philosophical, the warm-hearted, the optimistic, and the extroverted.

Whereas energy in the Pyramid disseminates from the vertex, energy in the Triangle travels in one direction, forming a circular pattern of energy within the confines of the Triangle. The Triangular component of Figure A allows for energies of the symbiotic relationship between architectural and human soul to travel jointly in a circular pattern in accordance with the dynamics of the energies of its structural being as previously mentioned. The gap at the peak of this Triangle allows for any and all negative energies of Psyche, Soul, and Spirit of both members of this symbiotic union to exit the relationship, as that energy passes by the exit in its cyclical pattern of travel within the Triangle. The discharging or releasing of positive vibes or energies through this gap is reflective of an inner that seeks the avoidance of reality.

The Cubistic component of this expression is reflective of an inner personality that is somewhat of a conformist, one whose outward actions and behaviors are in compliance with the current customs, rules, and principles of his surroundings.

Selection of this type of architectural expression containing Triangular and Cubistic components is most likely done by a reclusive, energetic escapist who possesses an abundance of positive energy to direct outwardly, yet lacks the mental and moral strength to venture out of the security and comfort of the conservatory Cube.

Our first Personifier, the Somersault, is a very simple release mechanism that allows one's outer-self to modify or personify any of these geometric shapes into architectural expressions that are tangible reflections of a persona's intangible inner-self. It is a voice for the influences of the persona that concern themselves with being independently rebellious. That seek to undo or reverse the natural order of things, more so for inquisitive reasons than for disruptive or uncooperative motives. The Somersault is an effective converter and release of negative feelings generated by being opposite or different in purpose or character. Use of the Somersault in personifying an expression reflects a persona that is strong, firm, and secure in its convictions despite the composition of its underlying values not being the norm of applicables or acceptables.

Figure B shows us what our sample expression looks like once release mechanism number 1, The Somersault, has been applied. Since the visual impact of the Cube has not changed, we are left with the

Figure B

same reflective expressional qualities of inner personalities associated with the Cubistic element of Figure A. What has changed is the visual impact of the triangular component of this architectural expression. Now the gap is on the bottom, serving as a port of entry for natural energy from the Earth instead of a escape hatch for the departure of negative energy.

A word about Earth's Energy. Our sun ejects large quantities of charged particles from its upper atmosphere consisting of plasma of high-energy electrons and protons commonly referred to as "Solar Wind." When this Solar Wind hits Earth, the effect is that of an enormous generator, charging all of Earth's atoms.

The being of the structure is not separate from the being of the inhabitant. The united being of structure and inhabitant isn't separate from the being of all living things, including Earth it-self. When Earth's Energy is absorbed into the confines of the Triangle, it too circulates alongside the Psyche, Soul, and Spirit of inhabitant and structure, an action that charges both parties of the symbiotic relationship with life-giving earthly nourishment. Alongside the symbiotic, what was Earth's Energy now becomes Life's Force within the architectural expression. It is Life's Force that ignites intrinsic elements, within the structure, of natural peace and tranquility. It is Life's Force that synchronizes earthly segments of our inner being, that which came from and belong to Earth, with Earth itself.

The architectural expression in Figure B would most likely ap-peal to inner convictions that crave unity with the physical earthly world, with causes, laws, and effects of all natural phenomena as-sociated with the universe. Organic personas and those with strong convictions on holistic ecology, as well as the down-to-earth, the sensible, and the realistic will also find rejuvenating energy and a intensification of inner peace as a result of inhabiting this expressive structure.

The next release mechanism that encourages the outer-self to have a say in modifying an expression once it has been selected by one's inner-self is release mechanism number 2, the Dispersion.

Figure C is our sample expression modified by first applying the Somersault, then modified again by applying a second Modifier, the Dispersion. The Dispersion is a voice for inner concerns dealing with the adventurous and the pioneering, the free-spirited and the unrestrained, the expansive, the liberal and the open-minded. The dispersion gives one's inner-self the sense of being able to sprawl or advance in any and all directions, of being able to travel or fan out. It creates a comfort zone that is an airy and spacious environment for both inhabitant and structure to interact in. It can be seen as a pacifier for the environmentalist or those seeking to be on a level plane with nature by allowing one to share Earth with Earth's creations.

Figure C

The Dispersion is of dual value. For in addition to its human worth, that of providing a specific means for one's inner-self to express a particular issue, it also possesses architectural worth. That of creating a broad, supportive base, a sort of platform or stage suitable for any number of inner psychic follies to express themselves on. Depending on the needs of the muffled inner-self, this versatile stage can take on the significance of a dramatic musical theater, a comical circus ring or perhaps something a little more physical, like a sports arena.

I myself have allowed my own inner-self the freedom to say uninhibitedly anything it wishes, in any way it deems appropriate, and it has said Figure D.

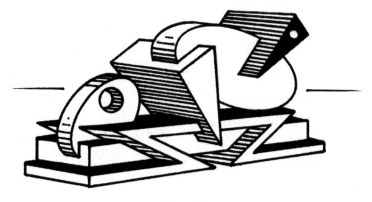

Figure D

It has said visually, in 3D, that which could not be said verbally. This process of modifying and then personifying by stacking on additional geometric shapes has lead to an architectural expression reflective of values and concerns that are of importance to my deepest inner-self and in need of being expressed openly. A ventilation of various art issues and convictions associated with my Psyche, Soul, and Spirit has taken place, easing stress and anxiety levels while at the same time promoting a positive mood and encouraging relaxation.

The combination of geometric shapes that can be stacked on or added to the expressive platform created by the use of the Dispersion are infinite. This release mechanism, that of piling them on higher and deeper, from top to bottom, left to right, as in Figure D, is referred to as Smorgasbording. Release mechanism number 3, Smorgasbording, is especially helpful in allowing a multitude of issues to be expressed at once. Two types of personas can benefit from Smorgasbording; those who have the need to express a variety of muffled issues belonging to one individual inner-self and those personas who are of multiple personalities. The use of a varied number of different geometric shapes by an individual persona

is reflective of characteristics that are associated with the posses-
sive, the accumulative, the demanding, the highly motivated, and
the enthusiastic. When only one or a limited number of the same
geometric shape is used repeatedly, over and over again, by an
individual persona, trapped inner issues associated with the obses-
sive, with always wanting more and never seeming to have enough,
find release. In the case of personas who are fortunate enough to
be blessed with multiple personalities, any and all of the principles
mentioned in this book, respective to the shape they refer to, apply.
Those individuals may wish to consult with their community Sha-
man or personal Guru to help them identify dominant issues of
their inner-selves. I, too, would be happy to assist those individuals in helping them successfully express their deepest inner-selves
in 3D form. Smorgasbording is an excellent way to confront the
confusion brought about by the warehousing of both dominant
issues as well as those of lesser value, but still of importance to
one's inner-self. The organizing and releasing of these issues and
passions will lead to an improvement in the alertness, focus, and
attention span of the outer-self.

Similar in application to the Dispersion is release mechanism
number 4, the Escalation. Both of these applications treat the fabric
of the structure with elasticity, the Dispersion stretching the structure horizontally and the Escalation stretching the structure verti-
cally. Escalation, Figure E, is reflective of inner issues relating to the
aggressive, the pompous, and the power hungry. Its use symbolizes
an inner that is fixed on its determination to successfully achieve,
a ladder climber who is idealistic and knows no top, a well-organized
perfectionist whose mission is to keep on systematically and
methodically achieving and perfecting. The higher the escalation of
his expressive trophy, the greater the intensity of satisfaction realized
by that inner-self.

Figure E

Both the Dispersion and the Escalation provide suitable canvases on which one's inner-self can portray issues that are lacking definite clarity, yet are gnawing and scratching away at its being. Use of the Escalation creates a vertical plane on which geometric shapes can be added or pasted to. Each addition to the side of an expression that has been escalated or placed on top of an expression that has been dispersed is an attempt by a confused and muffled inner to express itself as best it can in general terms. If an issue is presented generally, over and over again, an accurate feel of what is trying to be said can be achieved. Figure F is a example of Smorgasbording applied to Figure B after the Escalation has been applied.

Figure F

Escalation creates a vertical plane that is equally receptive of three other release mechanisms. Release mechanism number 5, the Spiking, release mechanism number 6, the Aperture, and release mechanism number 7, the Muralizing.

Figure G

Release mechanism number 5, the Spiking, Figure G, is reflective of inner issues associated with the intolerant, the jealous, the overly critical, and the vengeful. Spiking conveys a sense of persistent forcefulness, a uninhibited character that courageously plunges or dives right into matters of concern regardless of how many times it has failed at its attempts to achieve its end. Spiking is reflective of an inner-self that picks itself up, dusts itself off, and recovers quickly from failure or misfortune.

Figure G is our sample expression modified by way of release mechanism number 1, the Somersault, then modified again using release mechanism number 4, the Escalation, then personified using release mechanism number 5, the Spiking. The end result is an architectural expression of an inner that is a resilient achiever. One who tactically employs every and any means available to reach his end. He is comfortable with backstabbing and bears no remorse or harbors any resentment over succeeding through trickery or deceit.

Figure H

Appealing to a completely different set of inner issues is the Aperture. Figure H is our sample expression modified the same way Figure E was. However, instead of personifying it using the Spiking, it is personified using release mechanism number 6, the Aperture. The Aperture is a opening in our escalated expression that allows both air and light to pass through our sample expression. This opening permits the spiritual elements of the structure and the spiritual elements of nature to share each other's soulful energies by interacting with one another through the emission and absorption of each other's energies as light and air pass through the aperture. Aperturization allows for the spirit of the intangible and the spirit of the tangible to touch one another, achieving unity and oneness with nature by the architectural expression and the inhabitant on an intangible spiritual level. In the case of the Dispersion, this oneness with nature, architectural expression, and inhabitant is also achieved, but on a tangible plane. So Aperturization allows for the inhabitant's spirit to interact with nature on a spiritual, intangible plane and the Dispersion allows for the inhabitant's spirit to interact with nature on a physical, tangible plane. Aperturization is a prime example as to why these architectural expressions are not to be viewed as objects of architecture, but rather as release mechanisms for freeing trapped inner-issues, while at the same time bringing light to inner-selves that may lie hidden in darkness. Aperturization is especially useful in decompressing matters that have been harbored in darkness for a considerable length of time. Which raises the question, "Can architectural expression bring healing?" The answer is "Yes". In this instance, the Soul of the structure takes on the responsibility of absorbing negative energies from its significant other, the inhabitant, and releasing those energies into the Aperture. Once in the Aperture, those negative energies are swept away by wind and light to be discharged by nature via volcanoes, earthquakes, thunderstorms, etc. Positive energy absorbed by the structure through its interaction with nature is then absorbed by the inhabitant. Inner negative energies of the inhabitant have been released and replaced by positive energies and influences of nature. This new inner is now free to experience a sense of openness, calmness, peacefulness, and warmheartedness. In this symbiotic relationship, the Soul of the architectural expression cleanses, as well as purifies, the Psyche, Soul, and Spirit of the inhabitant, opening up a new avenue to travel on experiencing newfound joy in the revelation of life as he or she live in a casual, airy, carefree, open environment that is cultivating, as well as nurturing, a free-spirited, freedom-loving inner. Positive inner-issues that are well expressed through the use of the Aperture are those of the affectionate, the sensuous, the exhibitionist, the unconcerned, the spiritually orientated environmentalist, and those seeking accordance with the graceful delicacies of the celestial.

The last of the three release mechanisms that work well after Escalation is Muralization. When the image imprinted on the structure, by paint or by mosaic, covers the entire plane it is applied to, that plane is said to have been Muralized. When the image imprinted on that plane floats in space without background or supportive images, as in Figure I, that structure is said to have been Tattooed.

Figure I

Any emblem, cultural symbol, family crest, religious or political image, logo or insignia imprinted to a structure highly personifies that structure by tattooing it with an image that is of value and importance to the inhabitant's inner-self, while at the same time appealing to the inhabitant's outer-self. The worth of incorporating this dual appealing form of expression is immeasurable in terms of aesthetically harmonizing the symbiotic relationship between inhabitant and structure.

Use of the Tattoo reflects an inner that is both communicative and eloquent, one that takes pride in its relationship to the significance of the applied Tattoo and what that Tattoo represents. This persona is absolutely clear on its identity and is secure in its relationship to that Tattoo, as well as its relationship as to what the Tattoo stands for. The usefulness of the Tattoo is incalculable when one must explicitly express inner-issues or concerns via images that are familiar to other members of its community.

Muralization differs from Tattooing in that the symbolic images of the Tattoo are familiar to both inhabitant and community, whereas the images of Muralization contain hidden meanings of which the inhabitant's outer-self may not completely understand the significance of those images. When one requires Magnum Expression, one should think Muralization.

I was once commissioned to paint a mural of a large white bird perched on a limb with wings spread, ready to take flight across a midwestern open plain. On another occasion I was commissioned to do a mural taking place the second before impact of a bird of prey, swooping down with claws open, onto a small animal.

The white bird taking off of a limb was commissioned by a white collar worker who was leaving his high-rise office in a big city to drive a refrigerated tractor trailer cross-country.

The bird of prey swooping down on a small animal was commissioned by the owner of a fairly large company that specialized in acquiring smaller, financially weak companies.

In both instances, the creators of these murals were unaware that they were portraying deep inner convictions and passions by way of images that contained symbolic meanings to that segment of their inner-selves responsible for the commissioning of these murals. In short, both of these gentlemen had allowed their deepest inner-selves to become Muralized. The opportunity to allow hidden inner-selves of other dimensions their chance to say visually what cannot be said verbally, through the use of the most versatile of all release mechanisms, Muralization, is one that should not be missed by anyone. There are no inner-issues or concerns, no passion or conflict, no matter how dormant or dominant, of Psyche, Soul, or Spirit that cannot be expressed through Muralization. It is for this reason that I firmly believe that all inner-selves seeking release or expression should Muralize at least one exterior wall of their architecturally expressive structure by way of a mosaic and at least one interior wall via a hand-painted mural.

Now, do you want to venture down new paths of exploratory expression? Then say hello to release mechanism number 8, the Skew. Skewing makes apparent the endless possibilities of individual expression available to today's multidimensional inner-selves to authoritatively state their position in 3D. The aesthetic principle demonstrated by Skewing is that if an architectural expression is modified by use of the Escalation, then personified by Skewing it dramatically, the final expression will occupy air space off-center to its base. This action characterizes inner-issues and modes of being associated with the ambitious, the cunningly defiant, and courageous daredevilishness. High stakes risk takers, reckless decision makers, and those with a mischievous temperament will also find Skewing to be an effective release mechanism.

Figure J is our original expression modified via release mechanism number 2, the Somersault, then modified again using release mechanism number 4, the Escalation, then personified by applying release mechanism number 8, the Skew. Here, the use of the Skew has opened up another exploratory path of which to travel, seeking the most effective mode or means of release or expression: That of possibly adding a second geometric shape, supportive in nature, to our skewed expression. For the sake of opening up additional outlets of expression, any time two or more expressions are used, each shape is to be constructed of different materials or color in order to sharply contrast one shape with the other.

Figure J

For illustrative purposes, I have chosen to support the expression in Figure J with a secondary structure transparent in nature. The Transparency is release mechanism number 9.

Transparency, as in Figure K, eases inner feelings of being boxed in. Inner elements of the human persona portrayed by use of transparency are those of willingness to share, of warmhearted hospitality, of the candid and the straightforward, the extroverted and the exhibitionist. Claustrophobic issues and anxious feelings of being tense or stressed as a result of being fenced in or confined at work, or some other area of life outside one's dwelling, are also eased by way of the vast visual spaciousness that comes into being as a result of transparency.

Before we go any further, let me just say that in addition to failing to provide a suitable outlet for the multi inner dimensions of today's people to honorably and openly express themselves accurately, architecturally, the current Cubistic architecture of yesteryear also fails to allow creative energies and exploratory passions of today's architects to manifest their maximum potential in the architectural projects they take on.

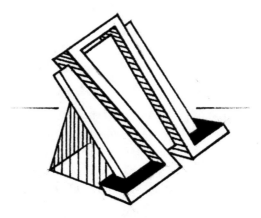

Figure K

Having said that, we now move on to the next release mechanism on our menu. The most awe-inspiring expressions of one's inner-self seem to come into existence by way of release mechanism number 10, the Helter Skelter. The world of computer graphics sometimes refers to this release mechanism as the "distortion." Intrinsic qualities of the Helter Skelter have their way of whimsically proportionalizing one's architectural expression, regardless of the number of modifications or the degree of those modifications to the expression. It is for that reason that the Helter Skelter works best when used last.

Figure L illustrates what our architectural expression in Figure B looks like after the application of release mechanism number 8, the Skew.

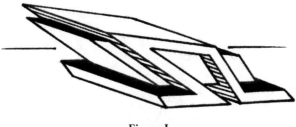

Figure L

Figure M is the application of release mechanism number 10, the Helter Skelter, to Figure L. A two-step modification process of Figure B that has led to the creation of an architectural statement of fascination and bewilderment. A tangible expressive statement that tells the community that the inner energies and concerns of its inhabitant are those of an energetic individual, eccentric in nature, who is youthfully lived and constantly striving for betterment and individualism.

Figure M

The unusual, unbalanced peculiarities of architectural expression brought about through the use of the Helter Skelter are those of inner-selves that are seeking to express concerns that are non-conforming to any sacred principles; they are boisterous about their high self-esteem and their need to be distinctive. They are pleasure seekers. Impatient in matters of gratification, irrational in the formulation of their own principles, and compulsive in making decisions of importance. Although I have stated that the Helter Skelter works best when used last, it is important to once again call to your attention that since no two combinations of Psyche, Soul, and Spirit are alike, there is no sequential order in which to apply release mechanisms. Nor is it necessary to apply all release mechanisms; application of only a few release mechanisms in different sequence provides a wide range of architectural structures capable of expressing an even wider range of inner-issues. This process of select and jumble provides one's hidden inner of another dimension with an endless amount of architectural vocabulary with which to express itself openly and uninhibitedly. It is for this reason that I do not want the reader to feel that the Helter

Skelter *must* be used last or that the Dispersion *should* be used early on in order to create a broad platform on which to stack expressions higher and deeper. Feel free to use the Helter Skelter first or the Dispersion last.

Figure N is Figure B modified using release mechanism number 4, the Escalation, then modified again using release mechanism number 8, the Skew. It is then finalized by personifying with release mechanism number 5, the Spiking.

Figure N

Compare Figure K with Figure N. Both these expressions appear similar in structural composition, yet, by way of their visual individuality, bear no similarities to one another in the attitudes and passions of Psyche, Soul, and Spirit that they represent. In Figure K, use of release mechanism number 9, the Transparency, is reflective of an inner persona which is open and outward, honest and upfront in its actions, desires, and motives. The persona reflected in the architectural expression of Figure N differs from the persona reflected in Figure K by the way of the inner persona of Figure N electing to express itself through the use of release mechanism number 5, the Spiking. The inner persona reflected by the architectural expression of Figure N is that of one who is overly critical of himself and others, one who is intolerant of any incompetence on his part or on the part of others. The persona reflected by Figure N is persistent and constantly attempting to quietly achieve without drawing attention to itself. It is not as open or as honest as the persona who incorporates use of the Transparency in its expression.

Figure O is Figure H, which has been slightly altered structurally at the drawing board on the direction of a local Illuminati. It demonstrates the infinite number of architectural expressions that can surface once the underlying inner-self loses its inhibitions and steps out from the shadows of the hidden chambers of our unknown inner dimension of the unseen self.

Figure O

In an attempt to free as many imprisoned inners as possible, I ask the reader to allow its outer-self, that of the Brain, the Heart, and the Blood, to allow its inner counterpart, that of the Psyche, the Soul, and the Spirit, the freedom to express visually, using the architectural vocabulary presented in this book, that which cannot be expressed verbally. I also do encourage the smothered and muffled hidden inner-selves of today's people to stand up and make their presence known. I further ask the totality of the individual persona to take responsibility for every dimension of its being, the seen and the unseen, the tangible and the intangible, and to live up to that responsibility by expressing itself architecturally and allowing that persona to meet itself openly and in public, creating a long-lasting harmonious relationship between inner-self, outer-self, the architectural expression that hosts them, and the community they exist in. It is one thing to have a relationship that will be there when times are good; it's another thing to have a relationship that will be there with you when times are bad. The quality of the relationship between all elements of the relationship, in all dimensions of one's being, is the persona's most valuable asset, its reputation. That persona should judge its success by the degree of inner peace that the living being enjoys in its physical, tangible existence in the real world.

Having said that, I invite you to share your thoughts and opinions with me by writing to me at architectural_expressions@yahoo.com. I welcome your questions and comments regarding the converting or expressing of inner-issues as well as passions of your life beyond the five senses into physical unconventional architectural structures of architectural expressions.

THE EXPRESSIONIST HAS NOT MORE HONOR THAN THE EXPRESSION.

1

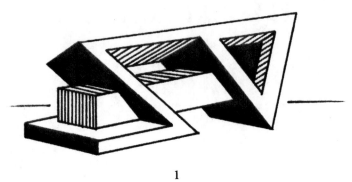

2

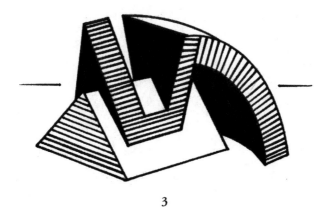

3

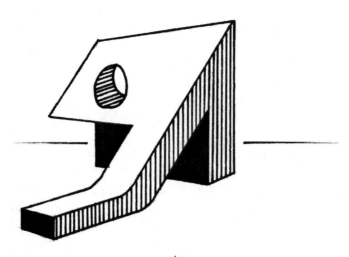

4

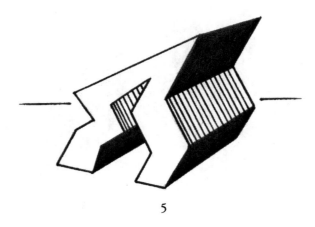

5

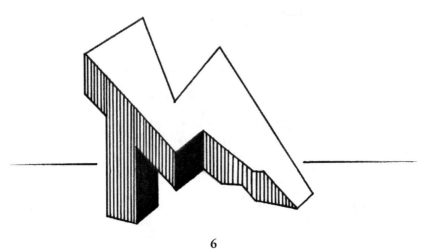

6

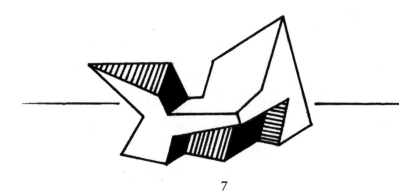

7

8

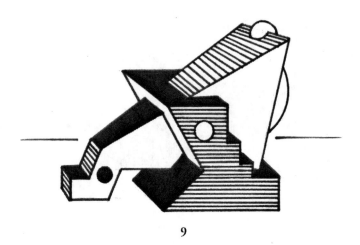

9

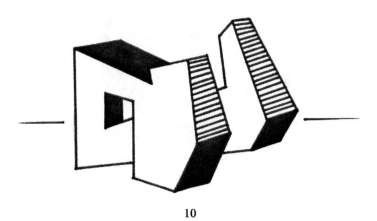

10

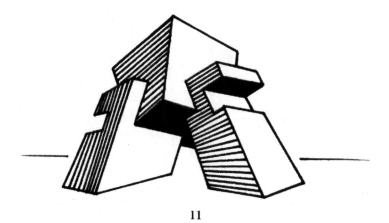

11

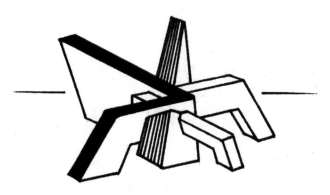

12

13

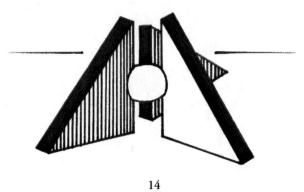

14

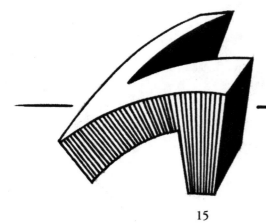

15

16

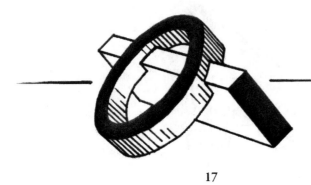

17

18

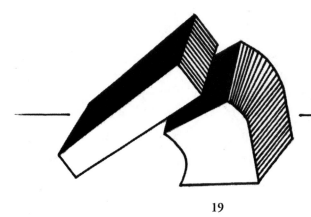

19

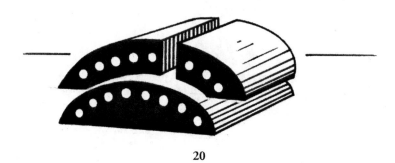

20

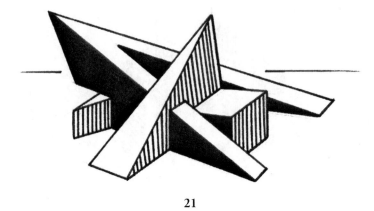

21

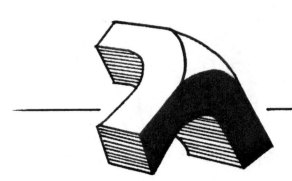

22

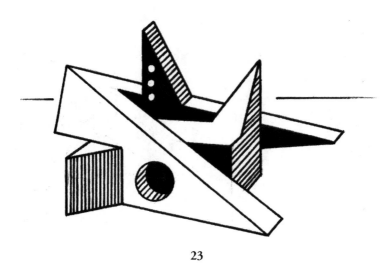

23

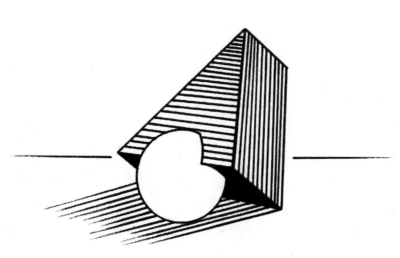

24

25

26

27

28

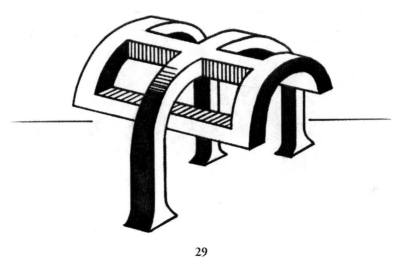

29

30

31

32

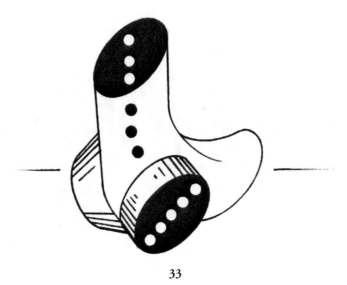

33

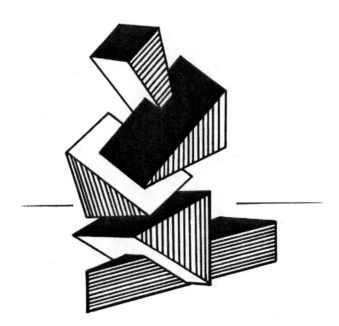

34

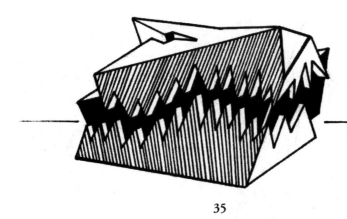

35

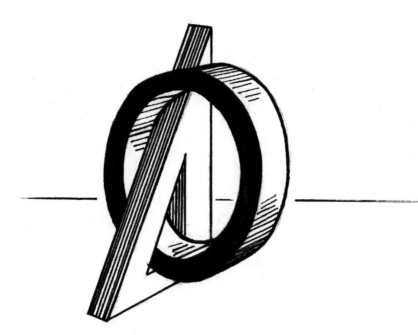

36

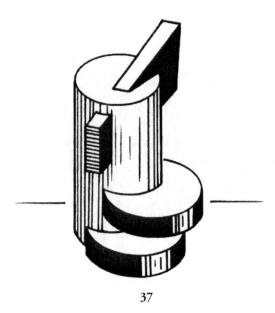

37

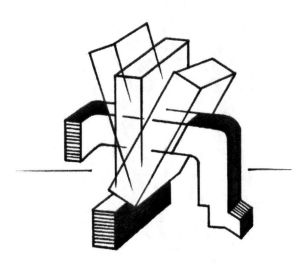

38

39

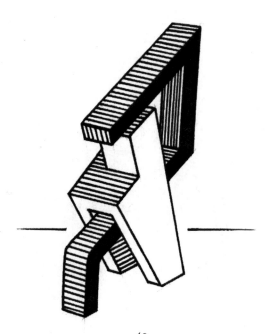

40

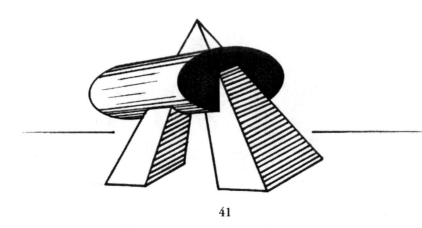

41

42

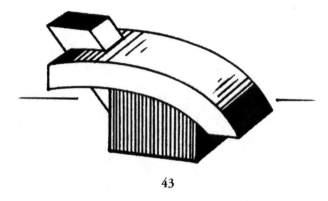

43

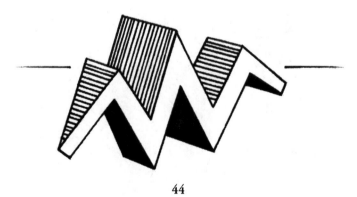

44

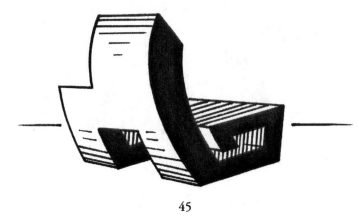

45

46

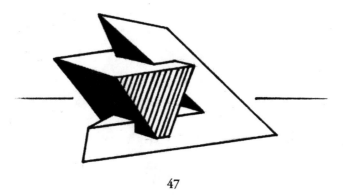

47

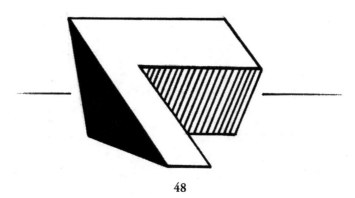

48

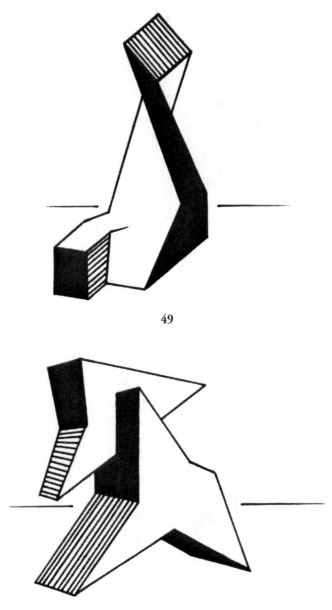

49

50

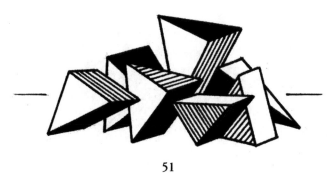

51

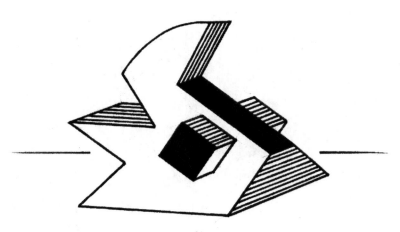

52

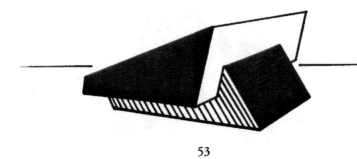

53

54

55

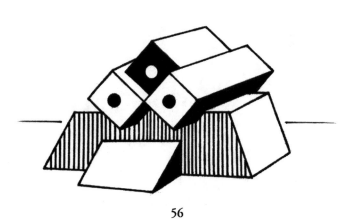

56

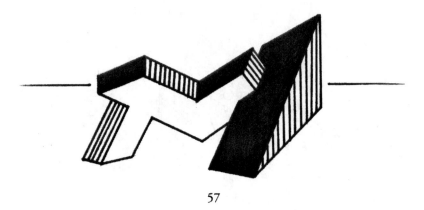

57

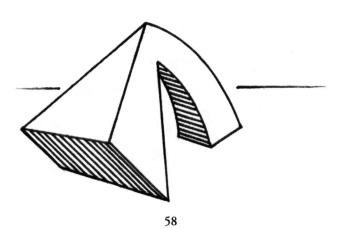

58

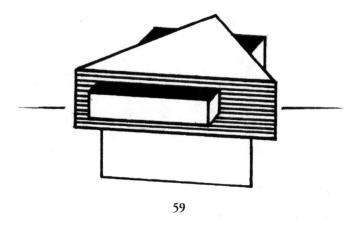

59

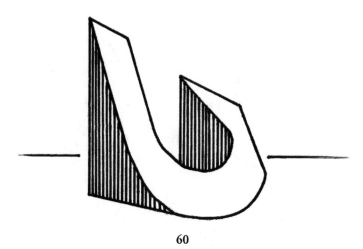

60

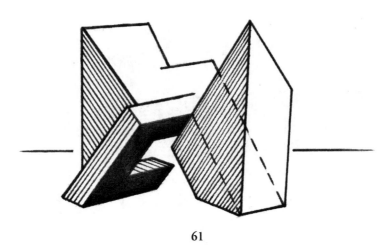

61

62

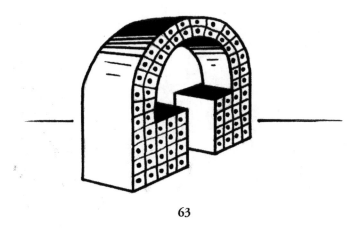

63

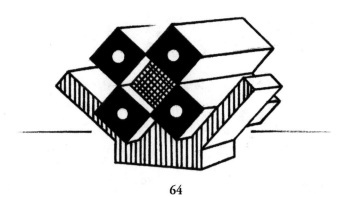

64

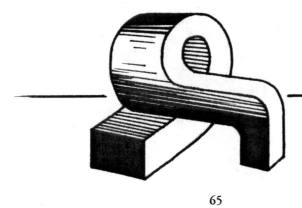

65

66

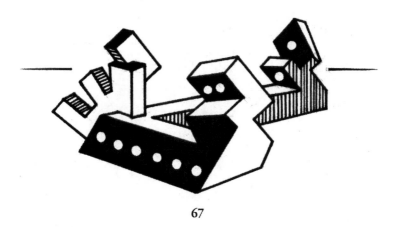

67

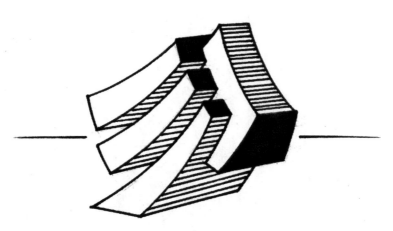

68

69

70

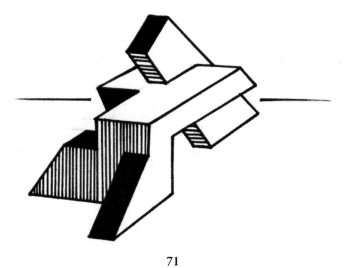

71

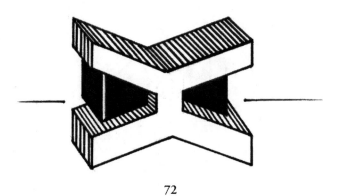

72

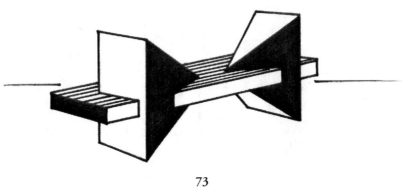

73

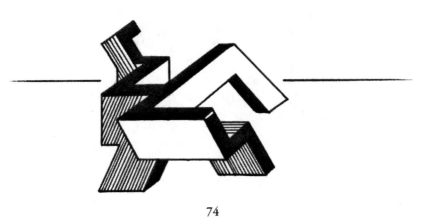

74

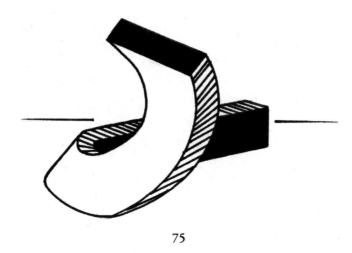

75

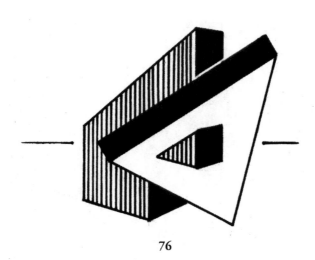

76

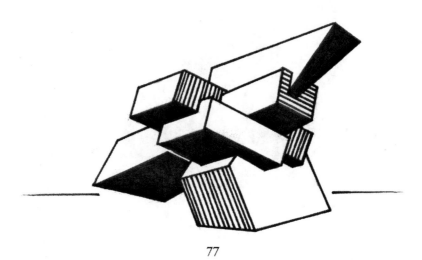

77

78

79

80

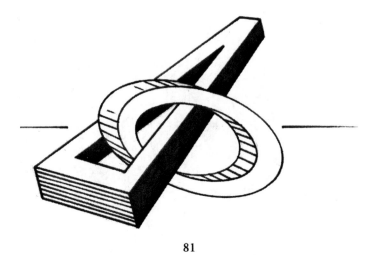

81

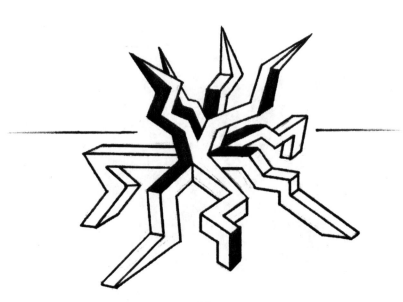

82

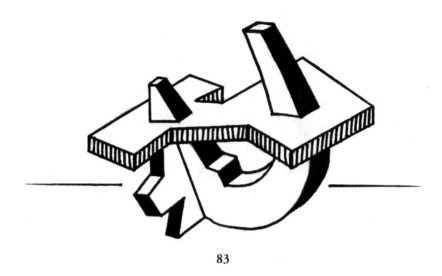

83

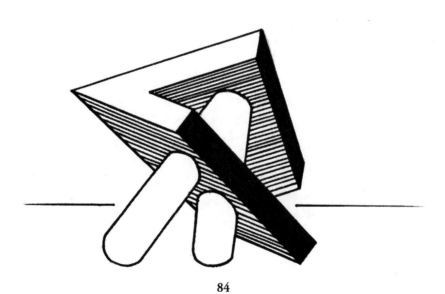

84

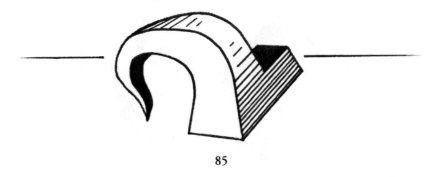

85

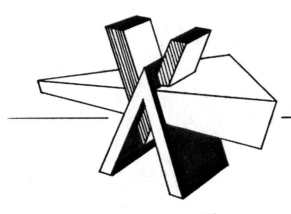

86

87

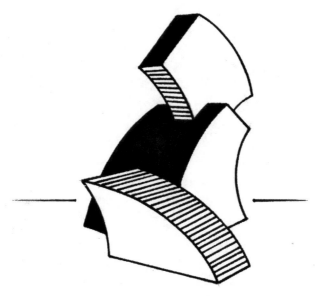

88

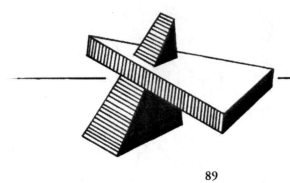

89

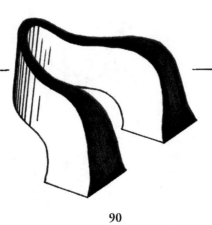

90

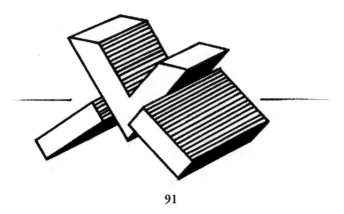

91

92

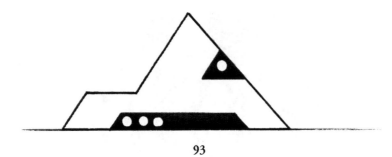

93

94

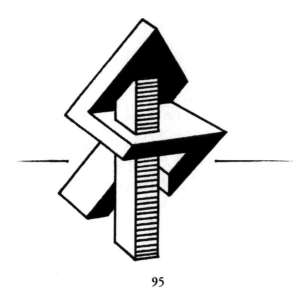

95

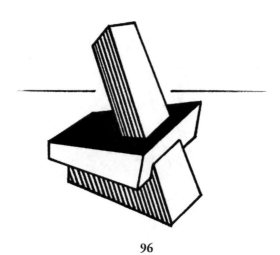

96

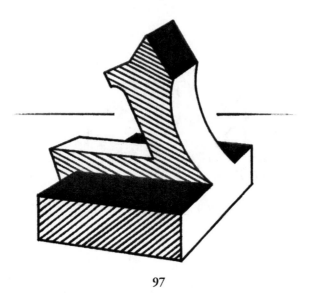

97

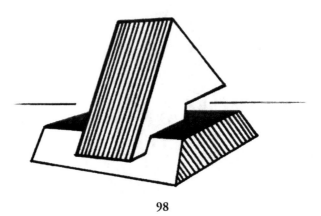

98

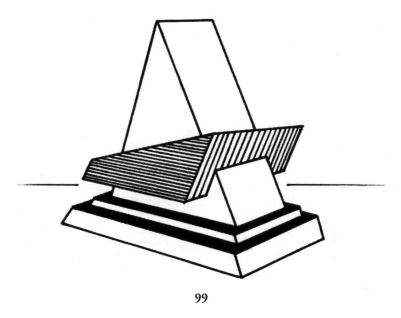

99

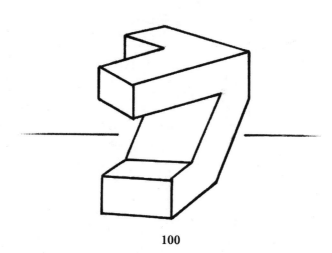

100

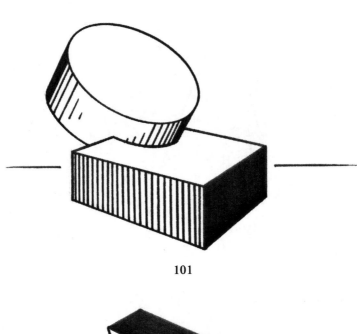

101

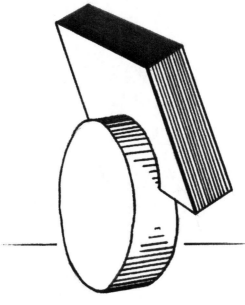

102

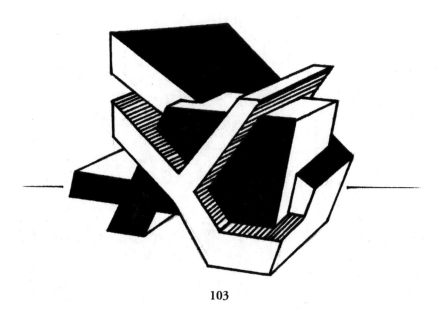

103

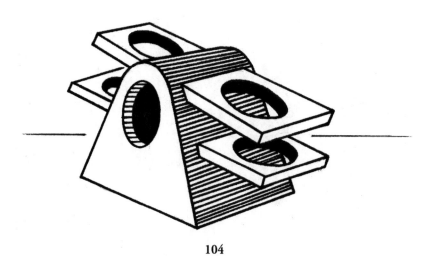

104

105

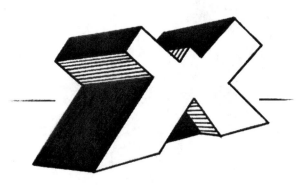

106

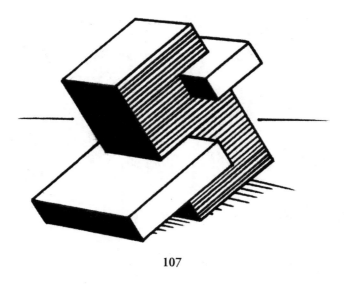

107

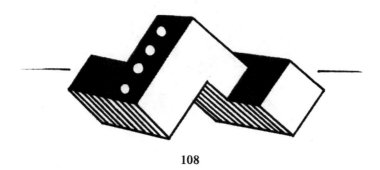

108

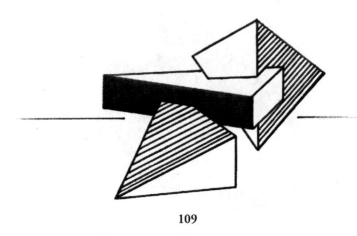

109

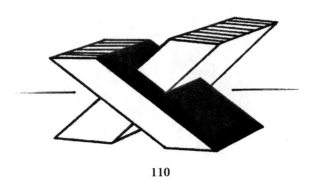

110

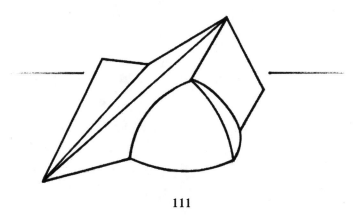

111

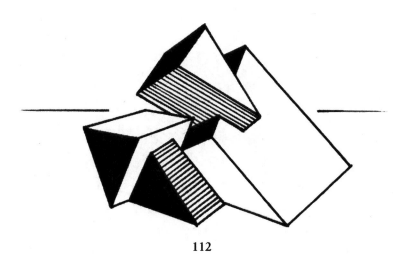

112

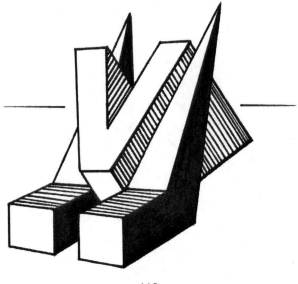

113

114

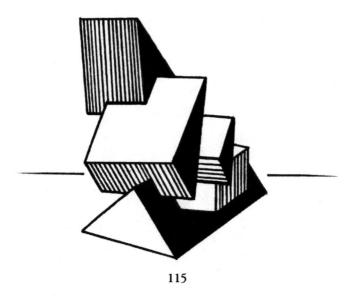

115

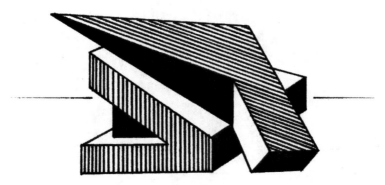

116

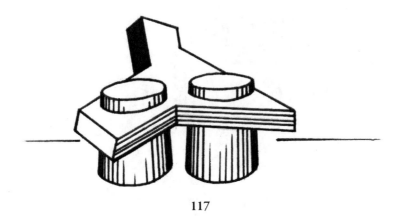

117

118

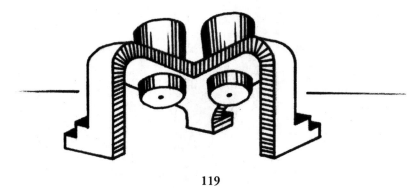

119

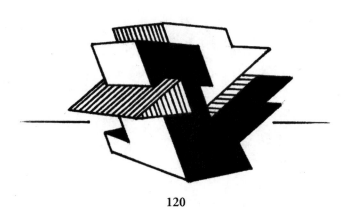

120

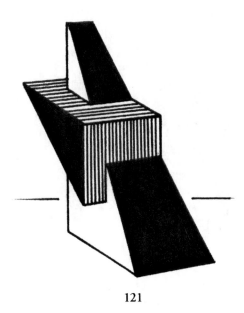

121

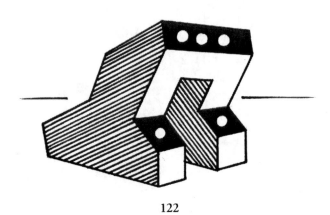

122

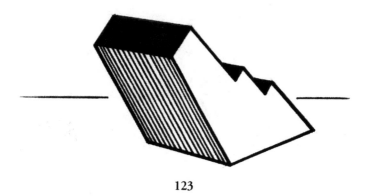

123

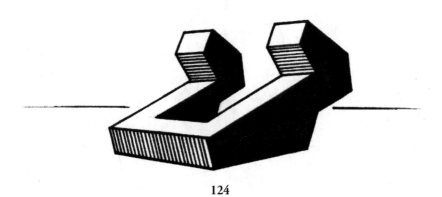

124

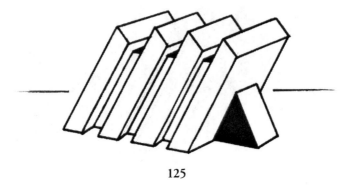

125

126

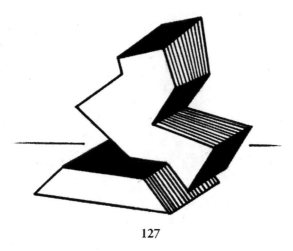

127

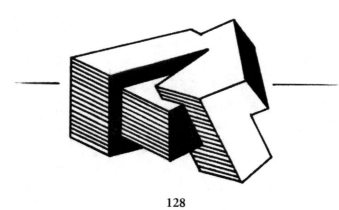

128

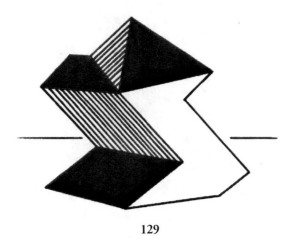

129

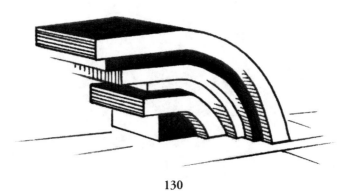

130

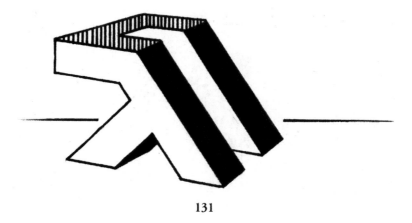

131

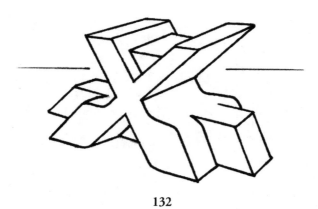

132

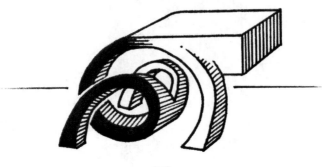

133

134

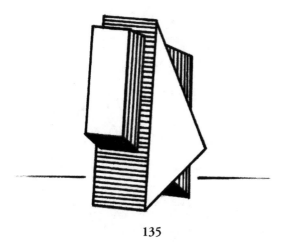

135

136

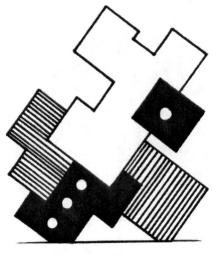

137

138

139

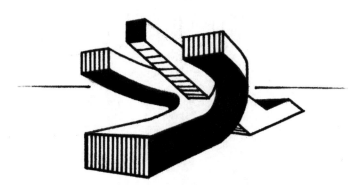

140

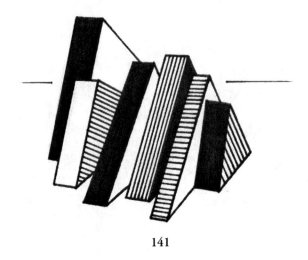

141

142

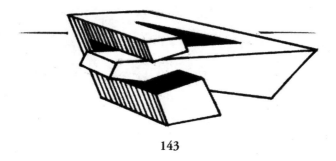

143

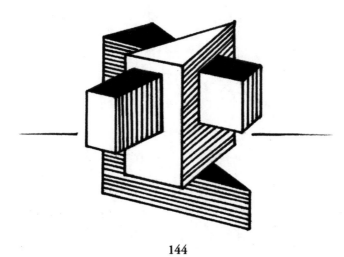

144

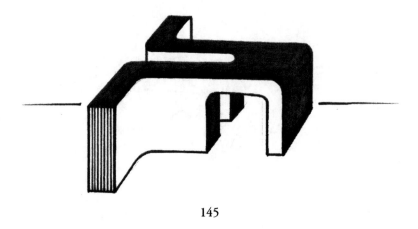

145

146

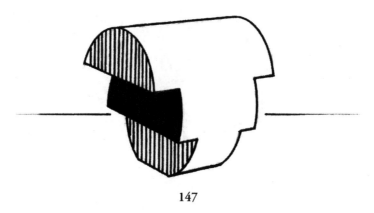

147

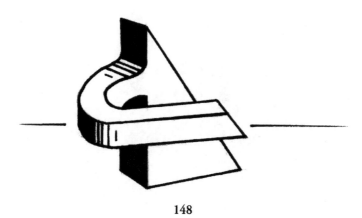

148

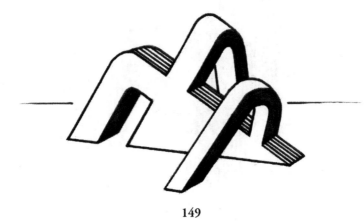

149

150

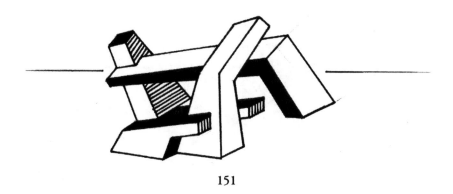

151

152

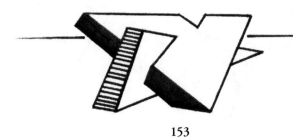

153

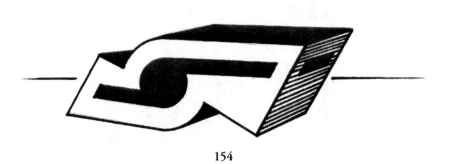

154

155

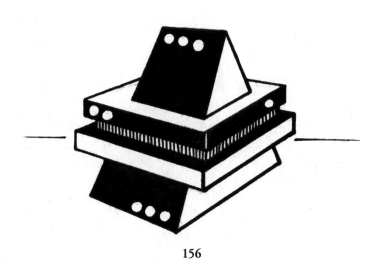

156

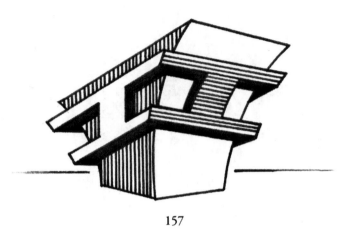

157

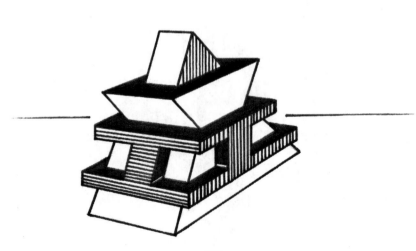

158

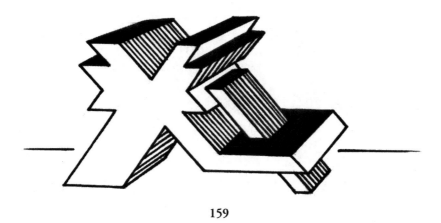

159

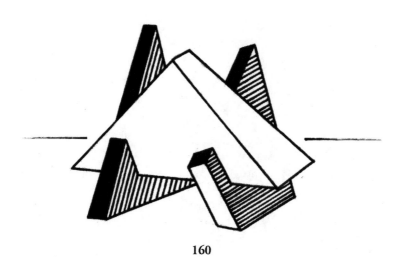

160

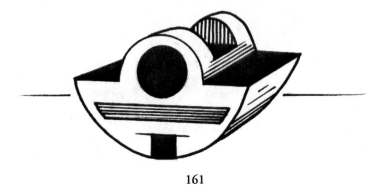

161

162

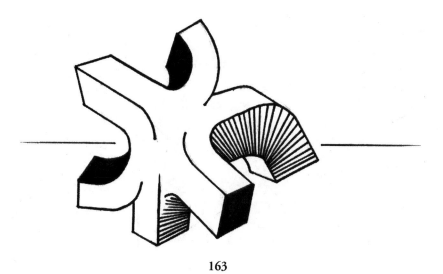

163

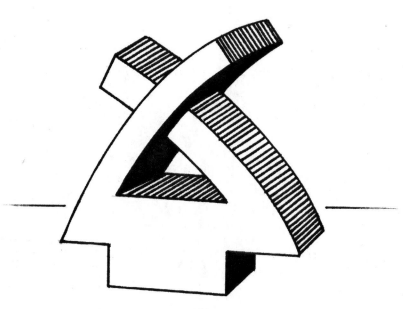

164

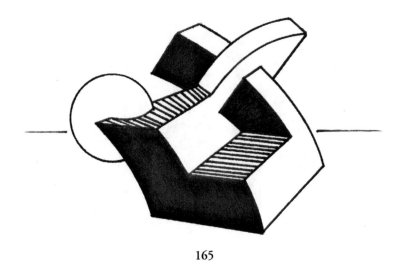

165

166

167

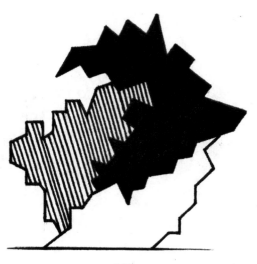

168

169

170

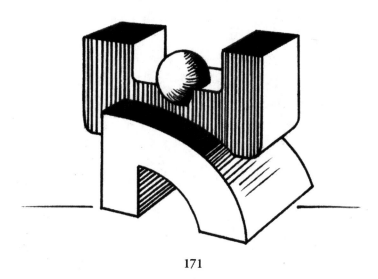

171

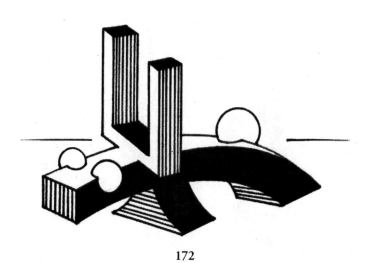

172

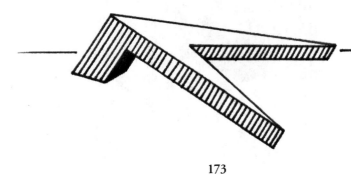

173

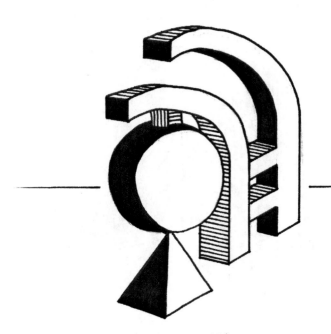

174

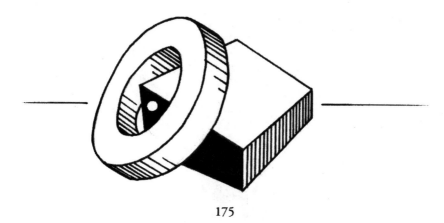

175

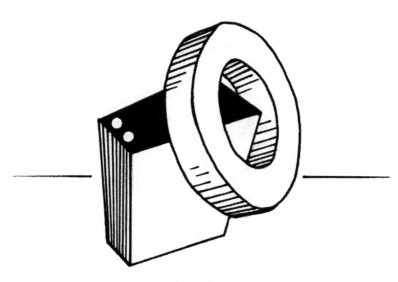

176

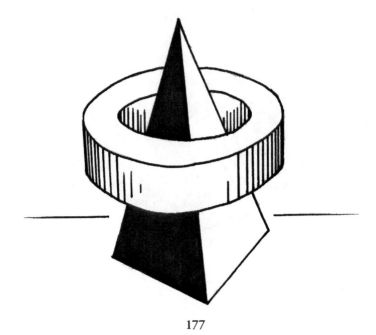

177

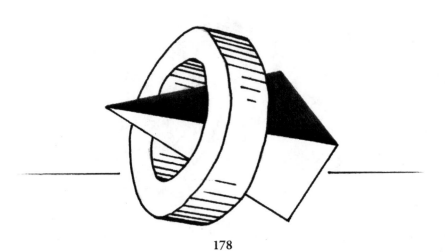

178

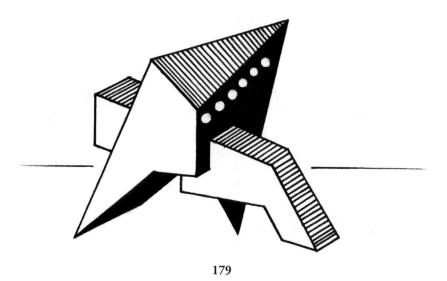

179

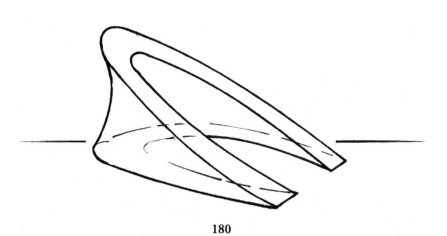

180

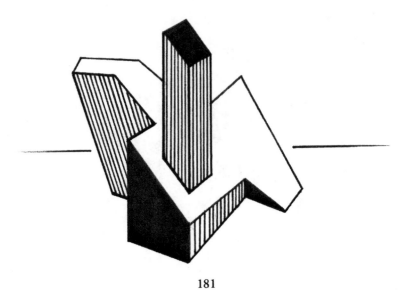

181

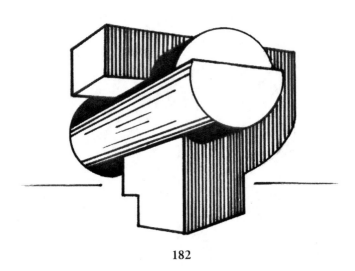

182

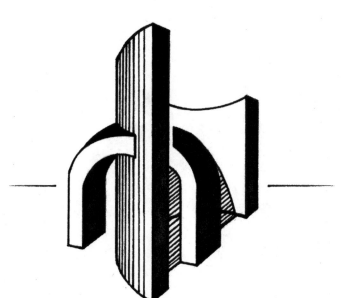

183

184

185

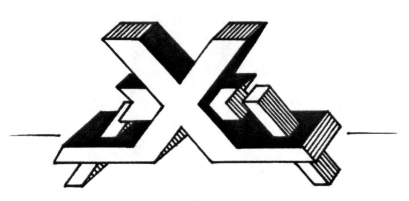

186

187

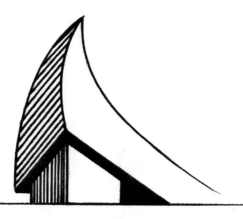

188

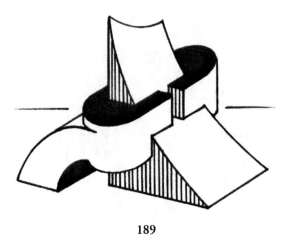

189

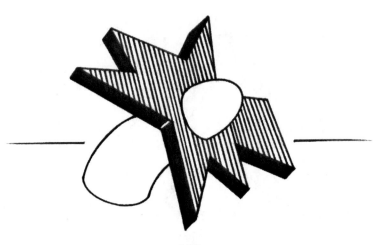

190

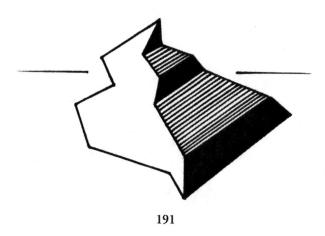

191

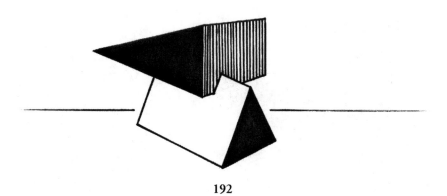

192

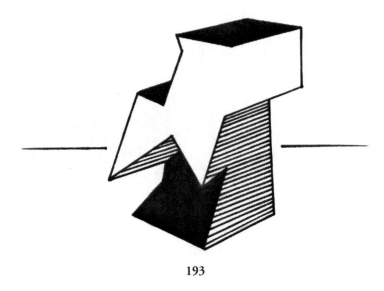

193

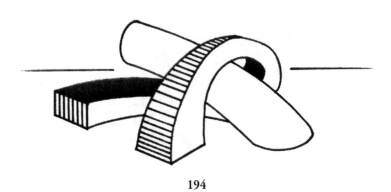

194

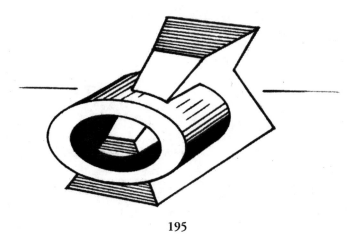

195

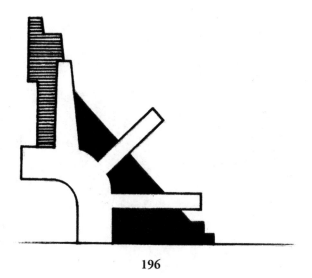

196

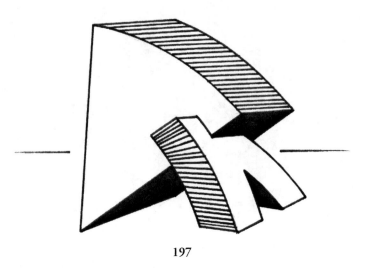

197

198

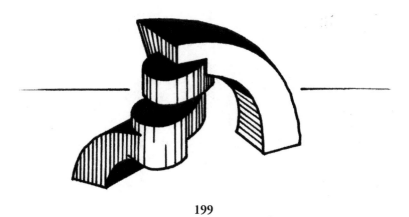

199

200

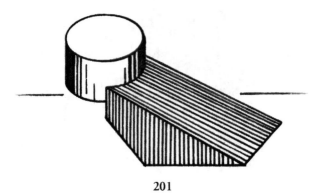

201

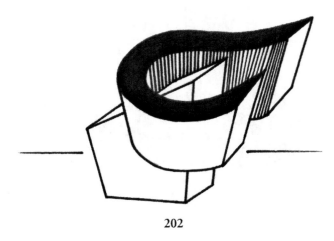

202

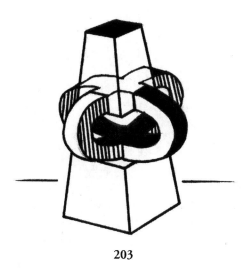

203

204

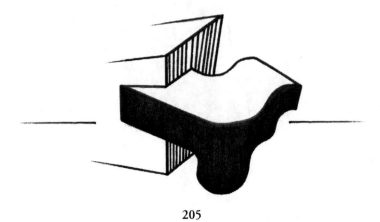

205

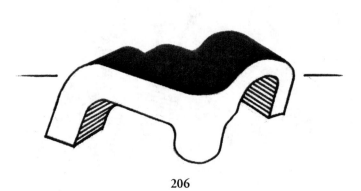

206

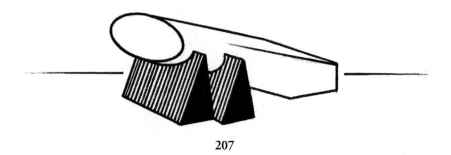

207

208

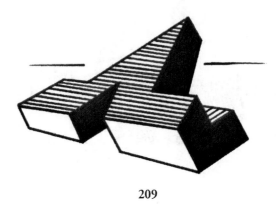

209

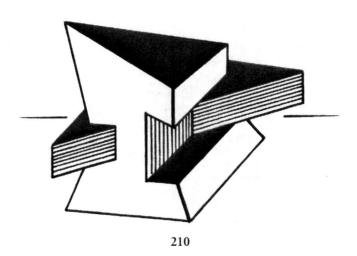

210

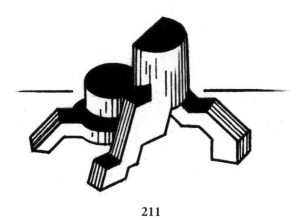

211

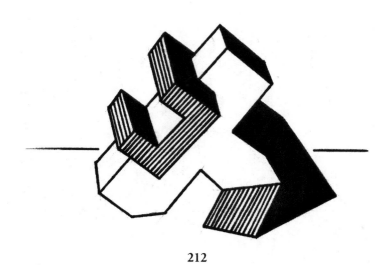

212

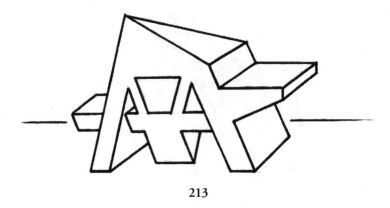

213

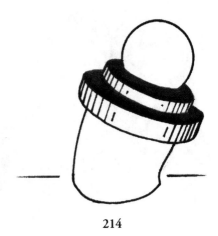

214

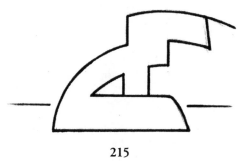

215

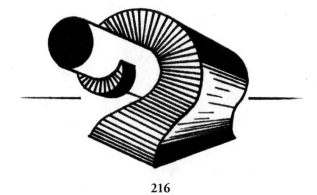

216

217

218

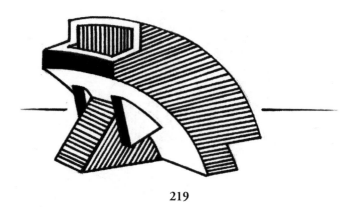

219

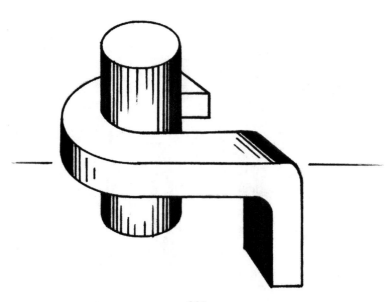

220

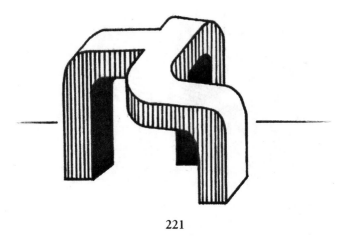

221

222

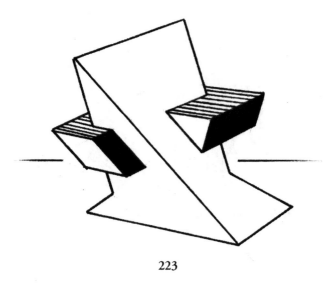

223

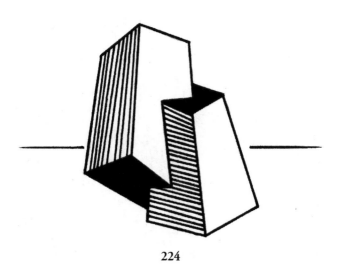

224

225

226

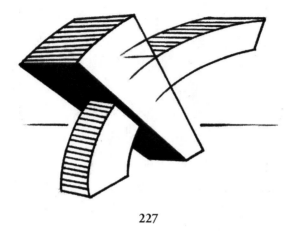

227

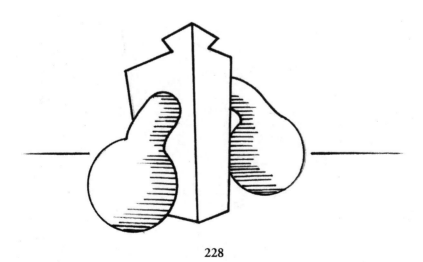

228

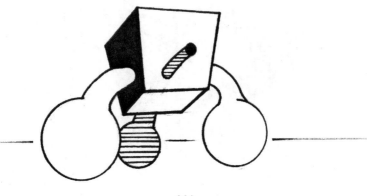

229

230

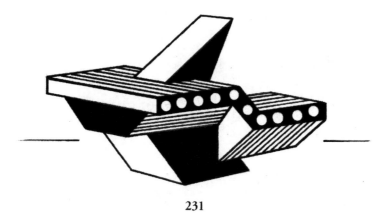

231

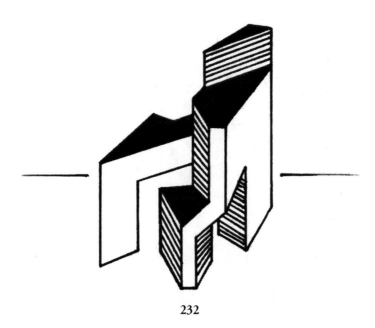

232

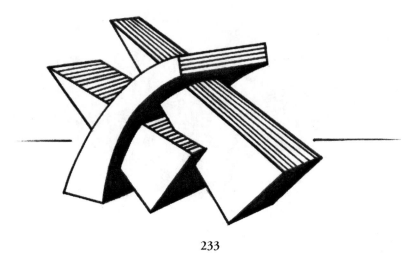

233

234

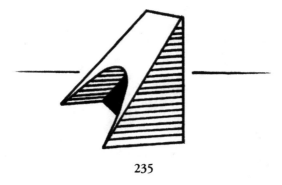

235

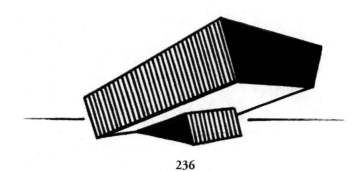

236

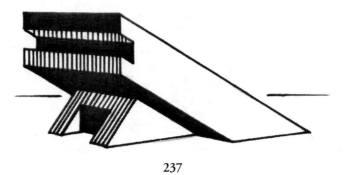

237

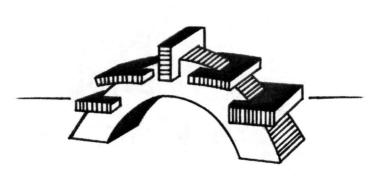

238

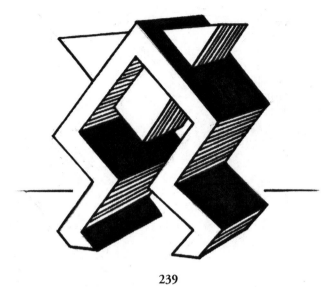

239

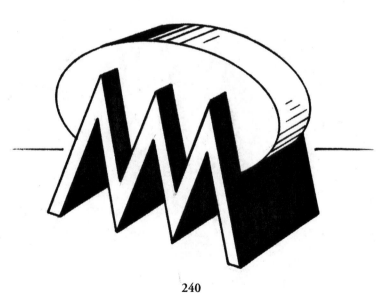

240

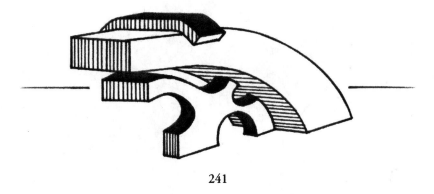

241

242

243

244

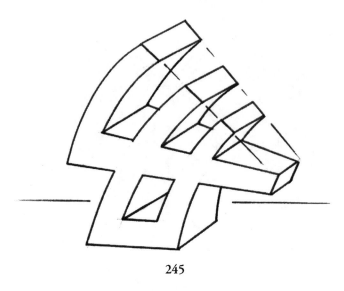

245

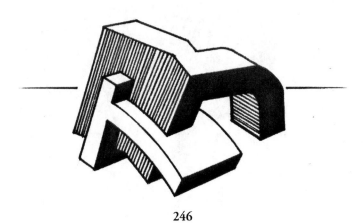

246

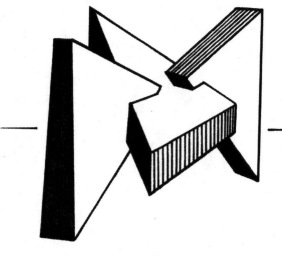

247

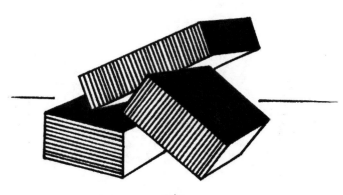

248

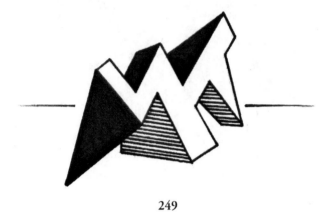

249

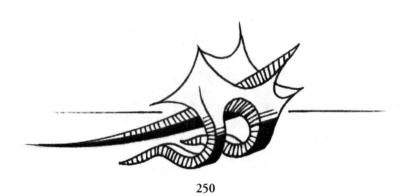

250

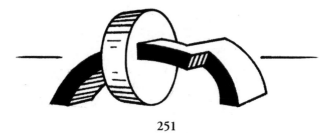

251

252

253

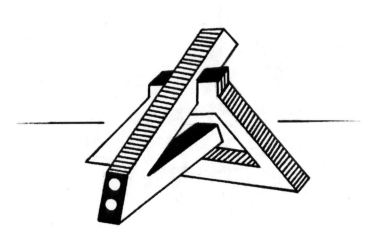

254

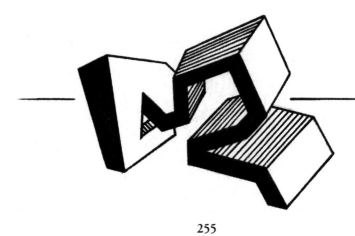

255

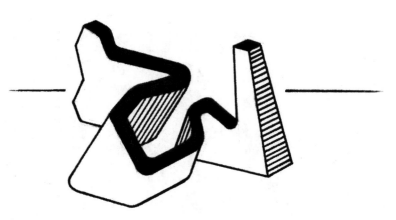

256

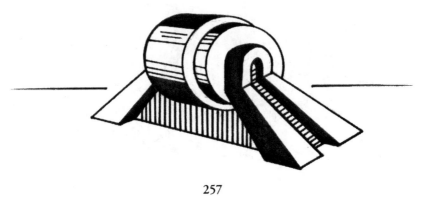

257

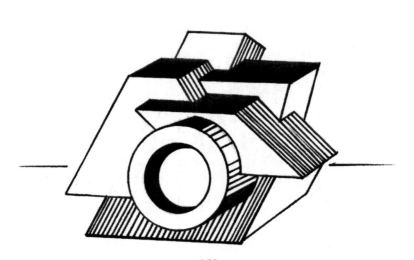

258

259

260

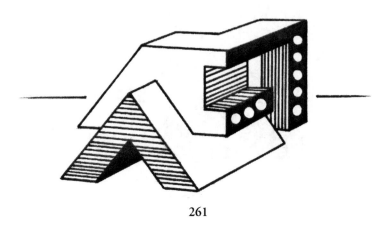

261

262

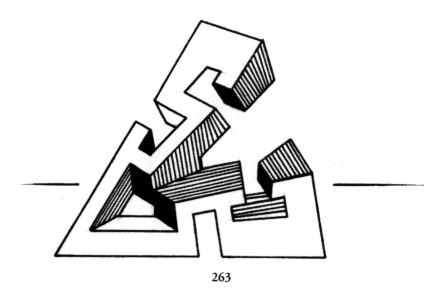

263

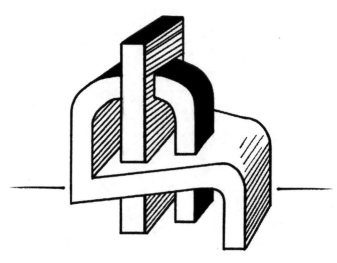

264

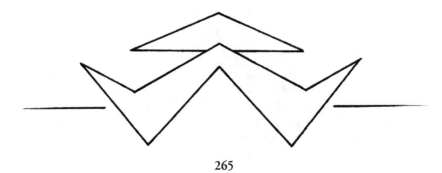

265

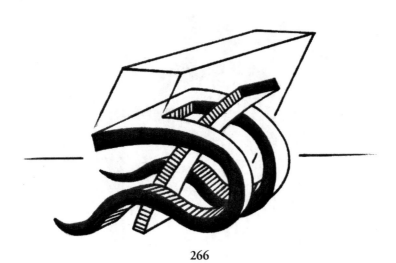

266

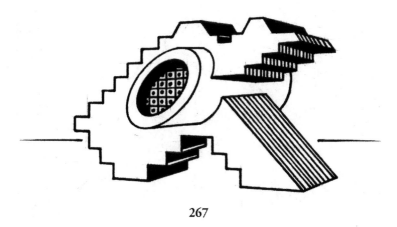

267

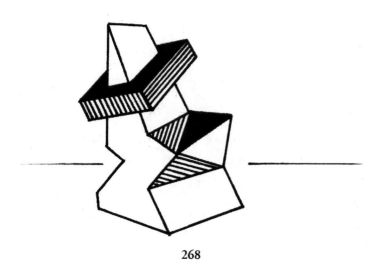

268

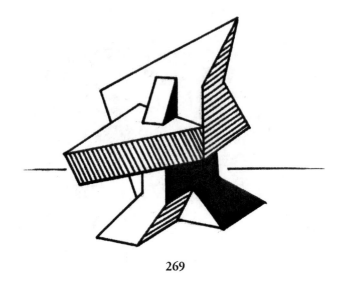

269

270

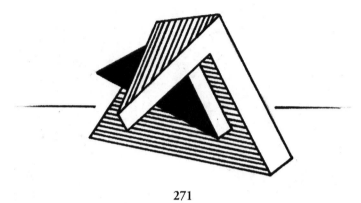

271

272

273

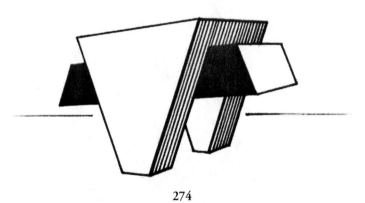

274

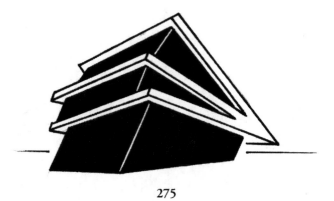

275

276

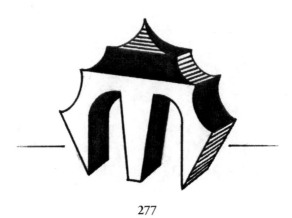

277

278

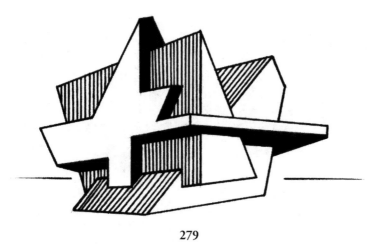

279

280

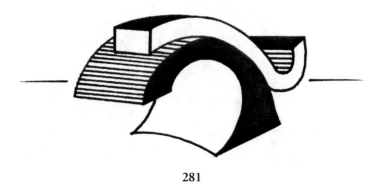

281

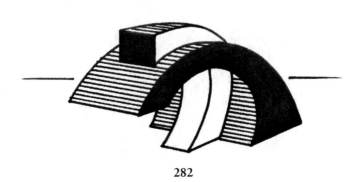

282

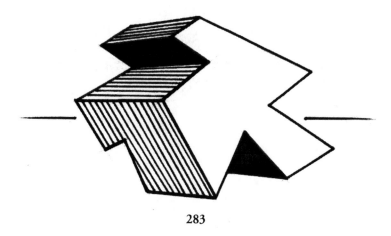

283

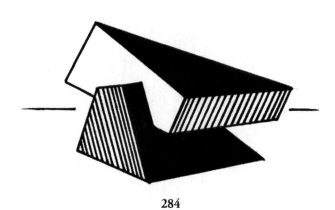

284

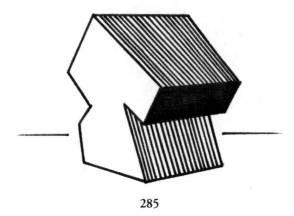

285

286

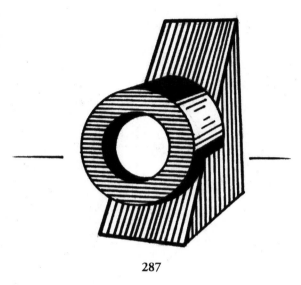

287

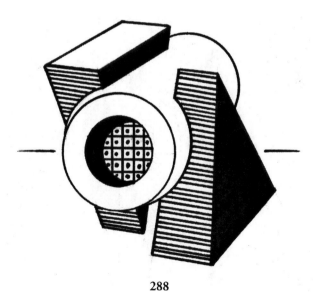

288

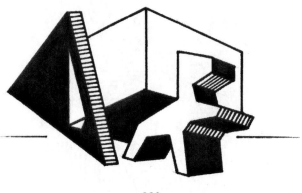

289

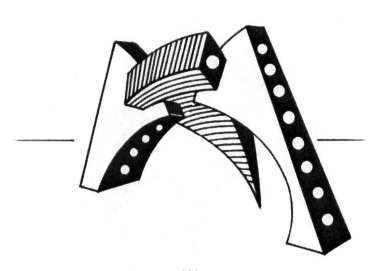

290

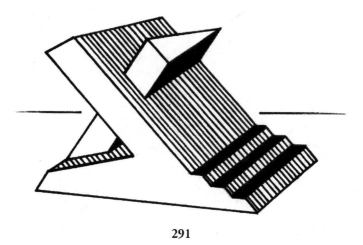

291

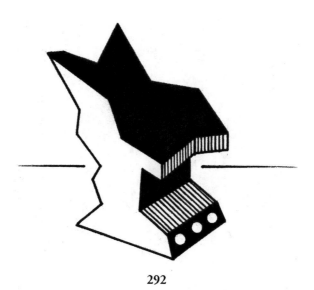

292

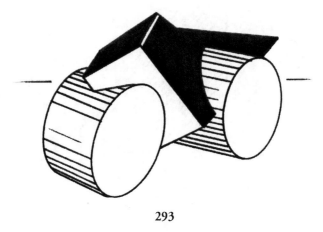

293

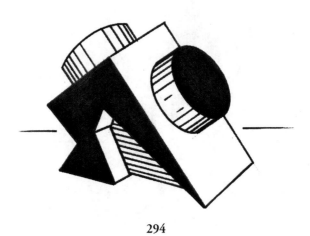

294

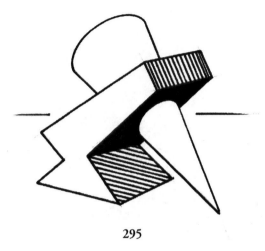

295

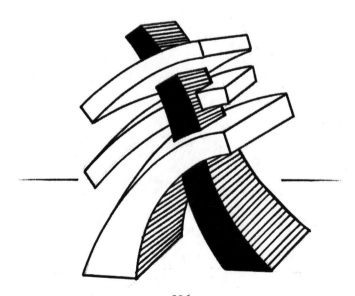

296

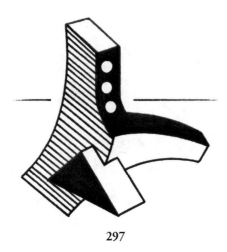

297

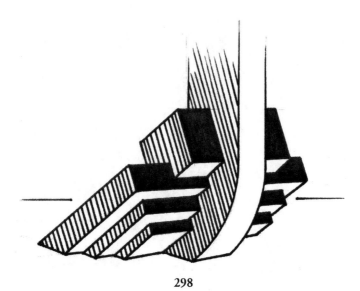

298

299

300

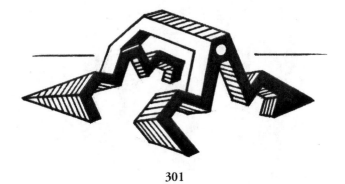

301

302

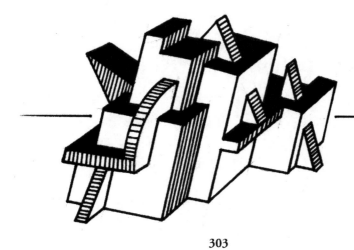

303

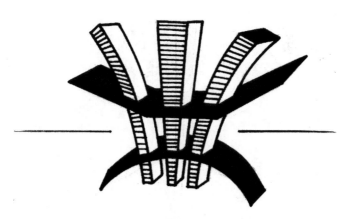

304

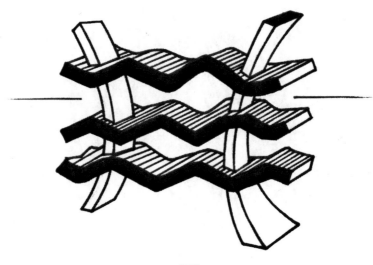

305

306

307

308

309

310

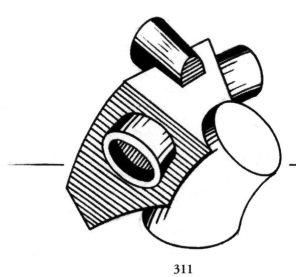

311

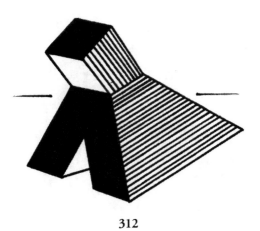

312

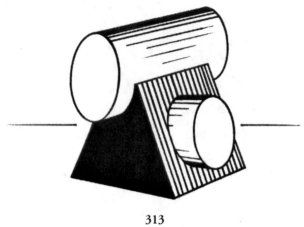

313

314

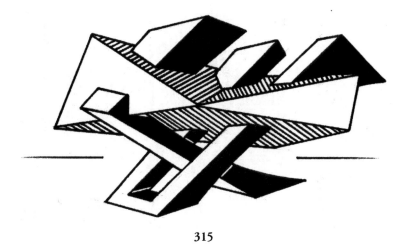

315

316

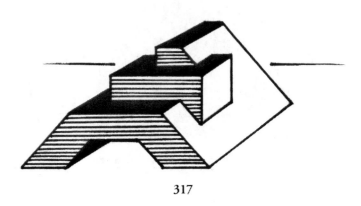

317

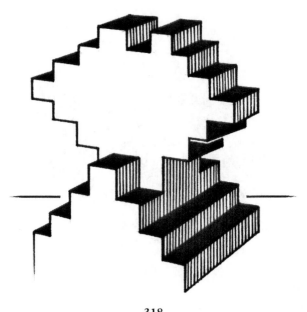

318

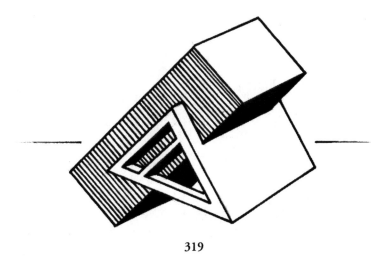

319

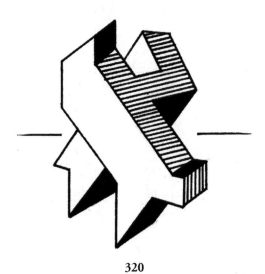

320

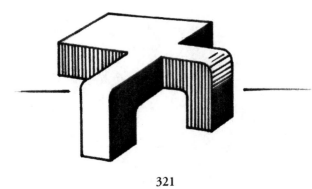

321

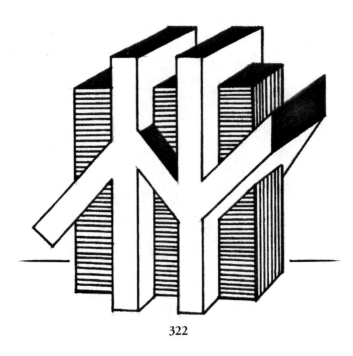

322

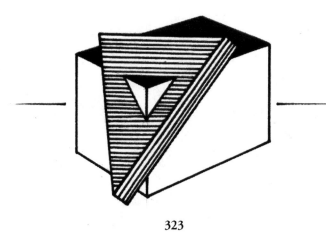

323

324

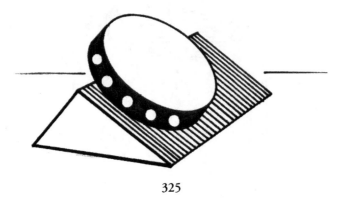

325

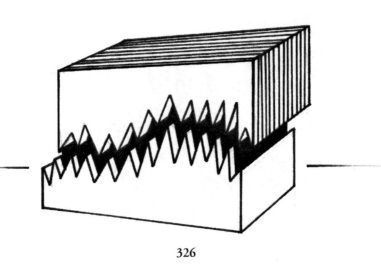

326

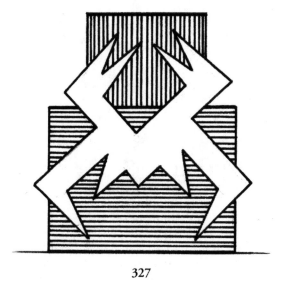

327

328

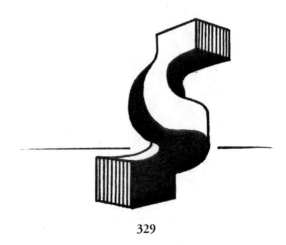

329

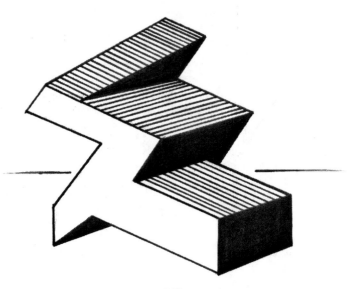

330

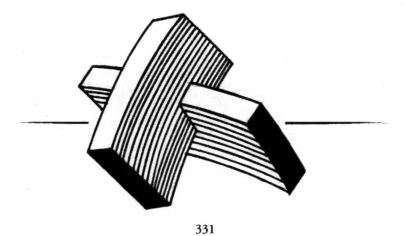

331

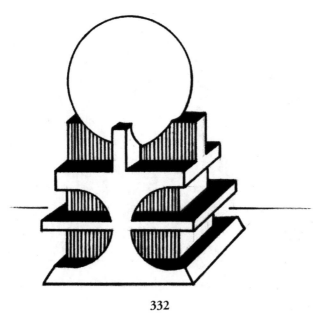

332

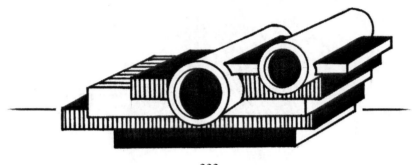

333

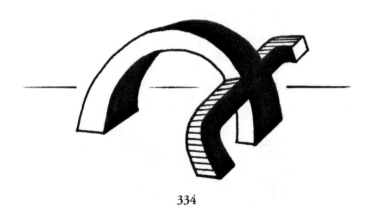

334

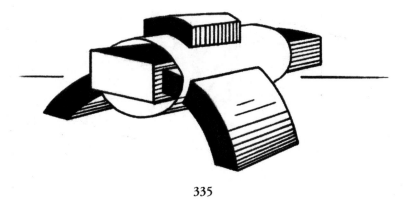

335

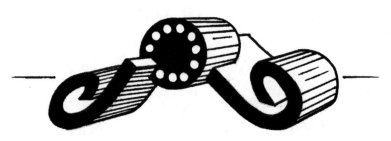

336

337

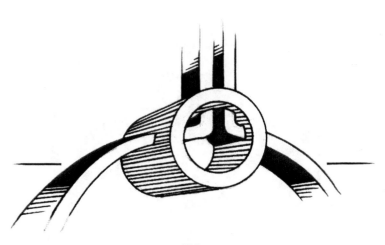

338

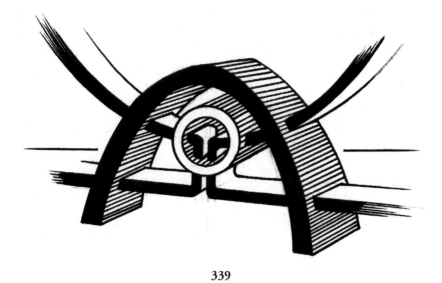

339

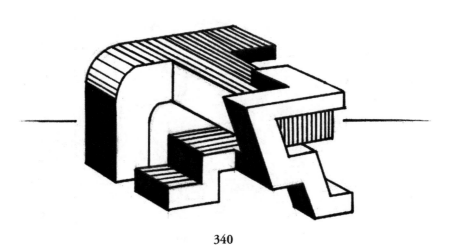

340

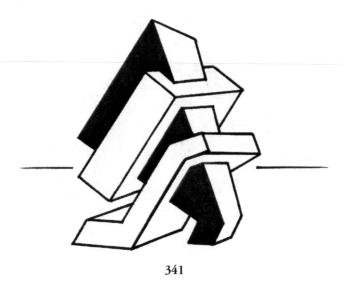

341

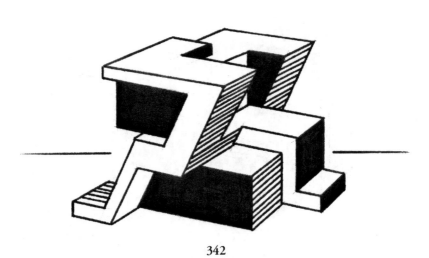

342

343

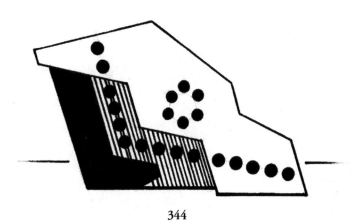

344

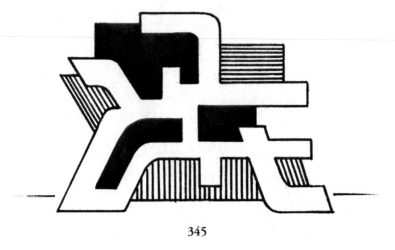

345

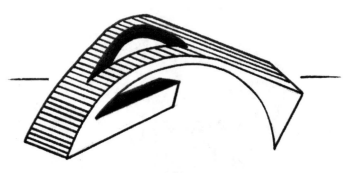

346

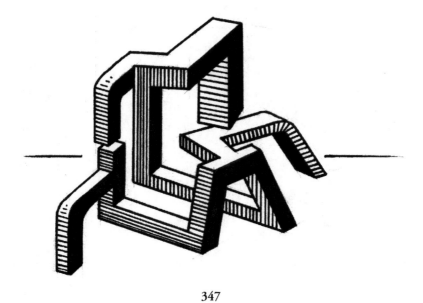

347

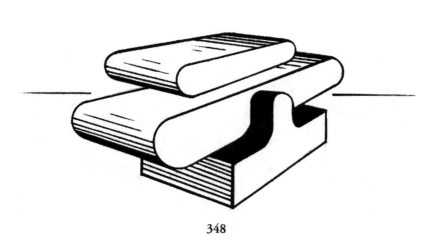

348

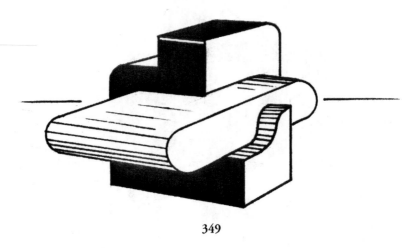

349

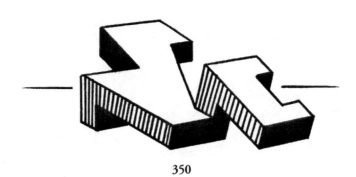

350

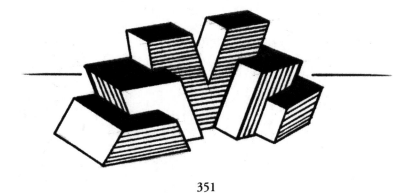

351

352

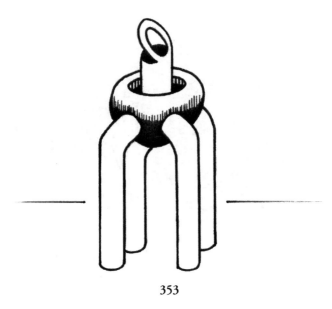

353

354

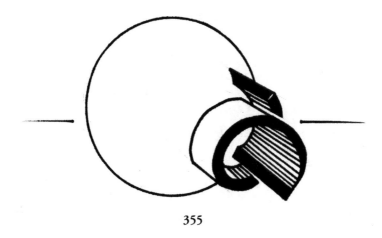

355

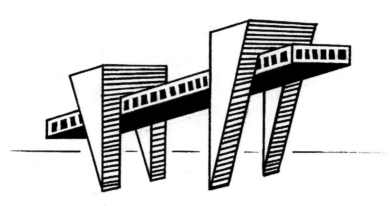

356

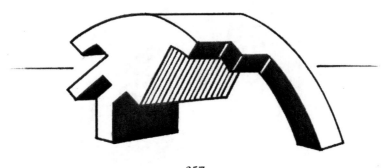

357

358

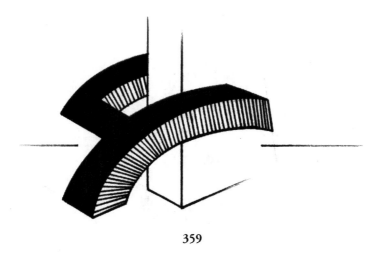

359

360

361

362

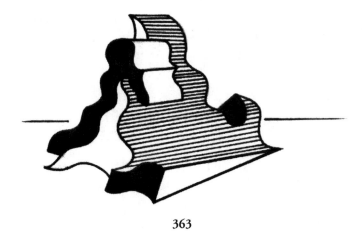

363

364

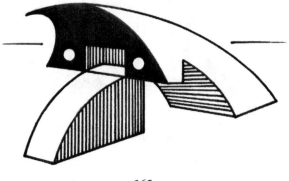

365

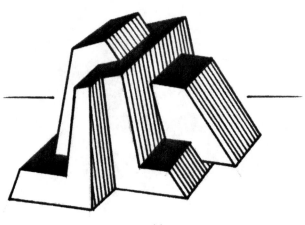

366

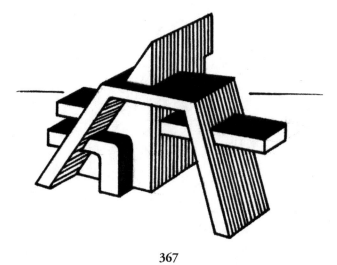

367

368

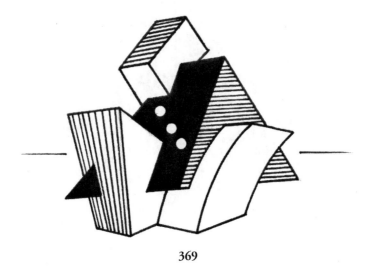

369

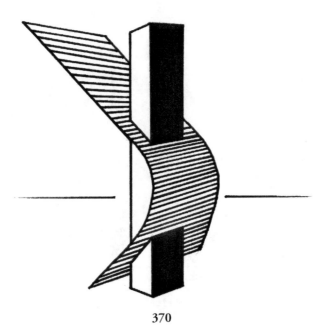

370

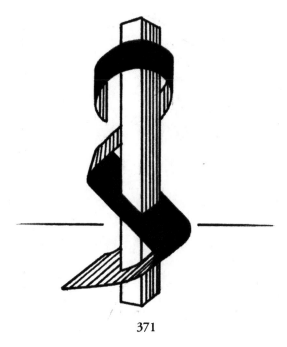

371

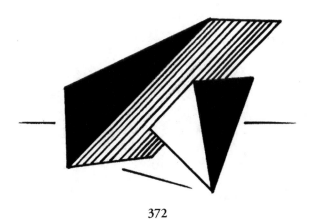

372

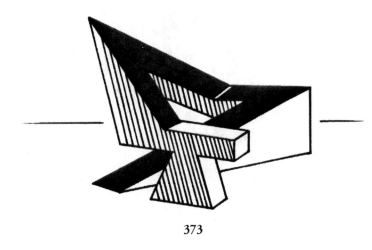

373

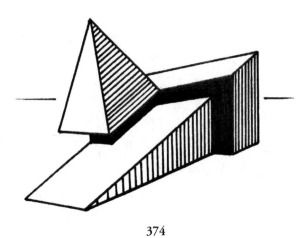

374

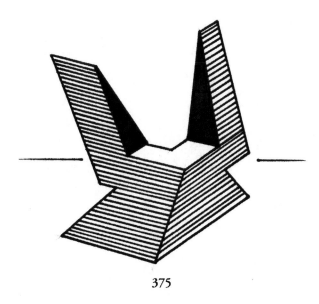

375

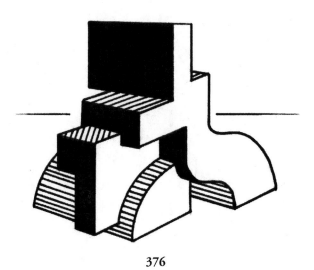

376

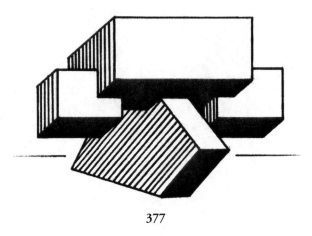

377

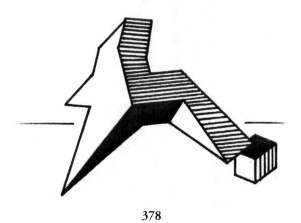

378

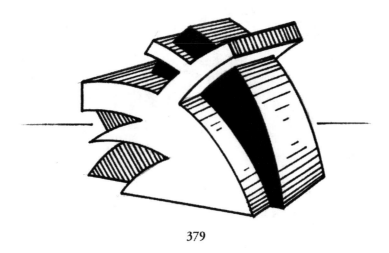

379

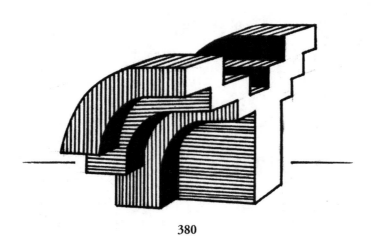

380

381

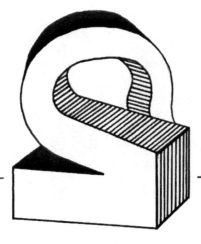

382

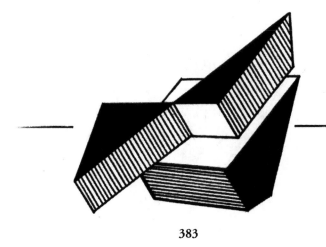

383

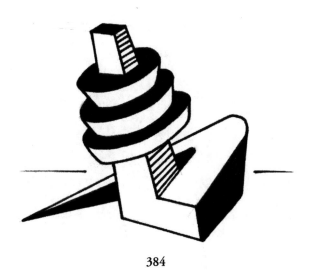

384

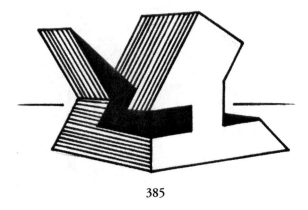

385

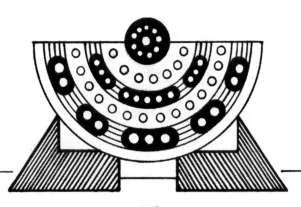

386

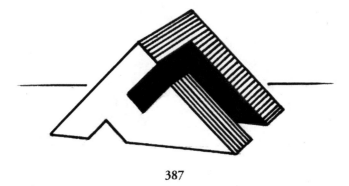

387

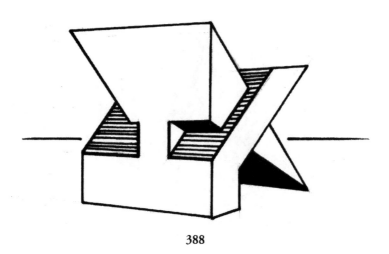

388

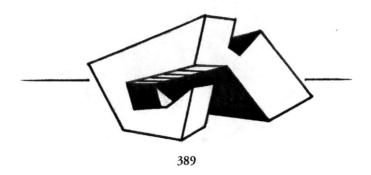

389

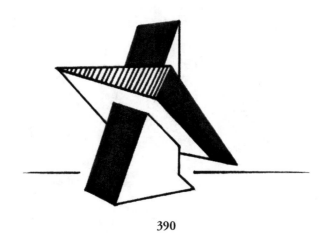

390

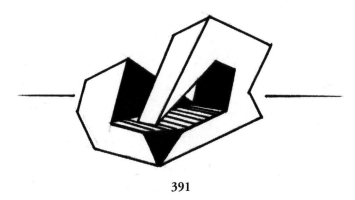

391

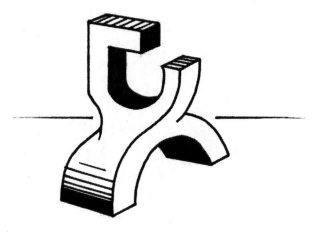

392

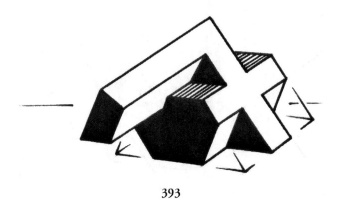

393

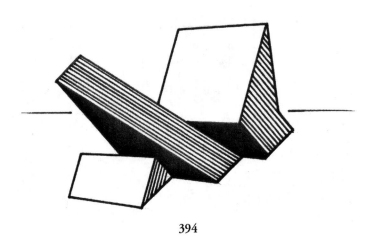

394

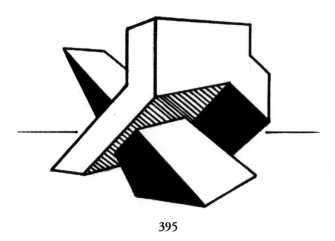

395

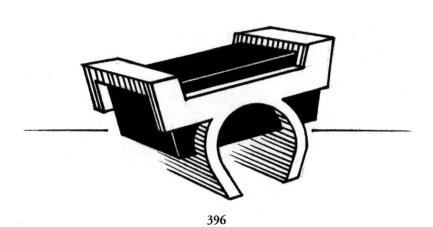

396

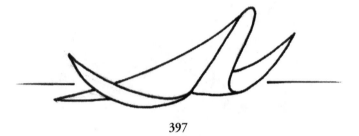

397

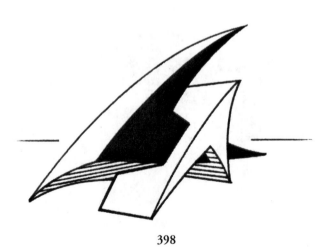

398

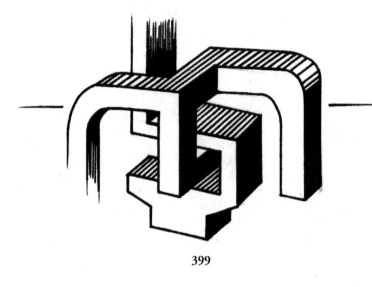

399

400

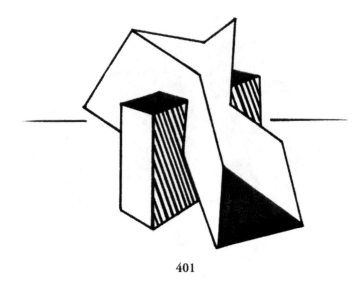

401

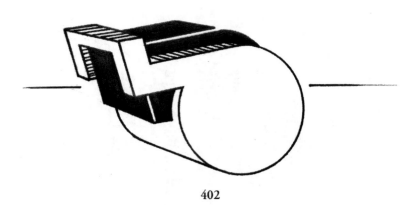

402

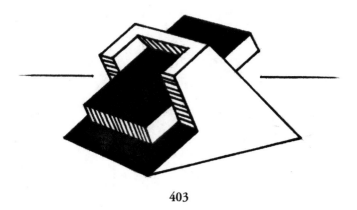

403

404

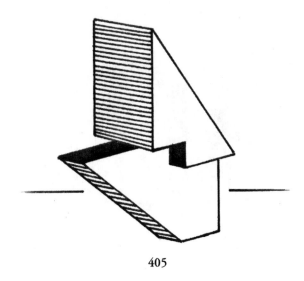

405

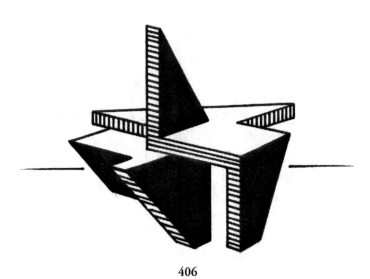

406

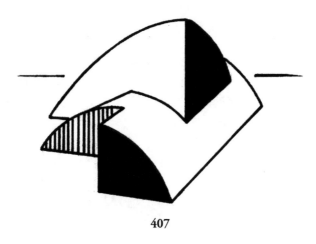

407

408

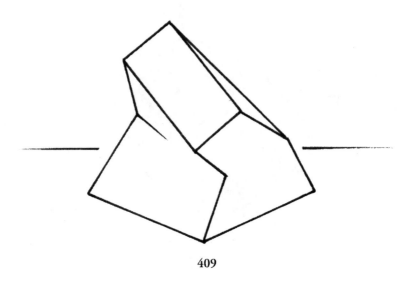

409

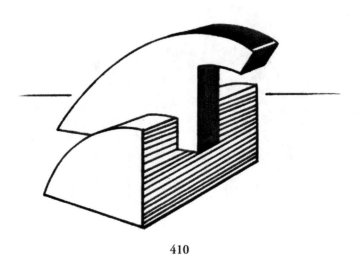

410

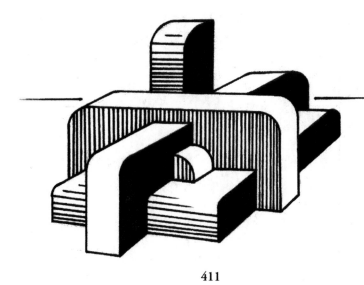

411

412

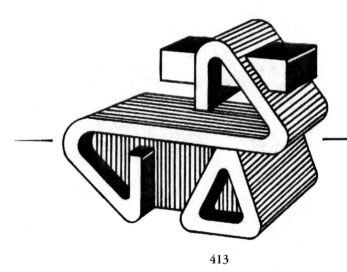

413

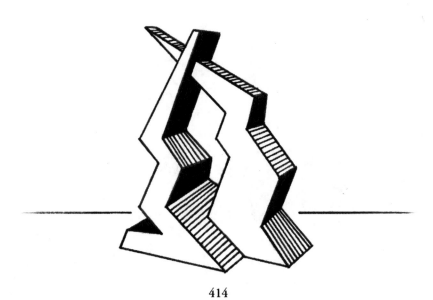

414

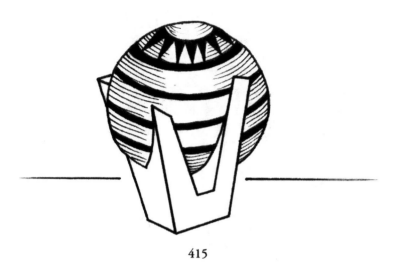

415

416

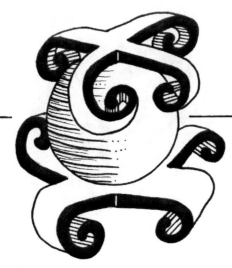

417

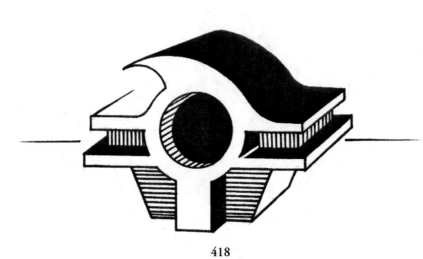

418

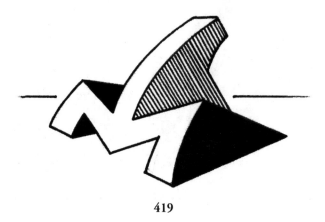

419

420

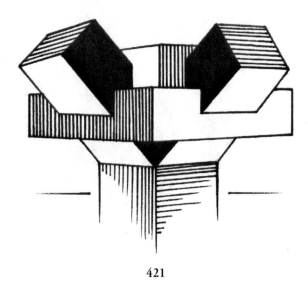

421

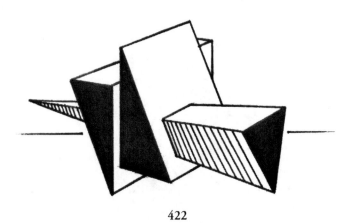

422

423

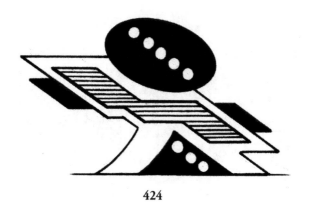

424

425

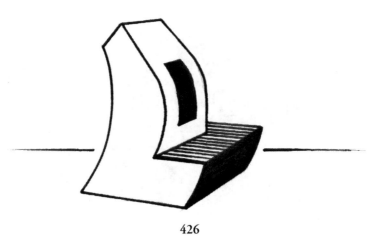

426

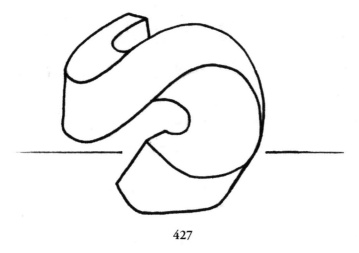

427

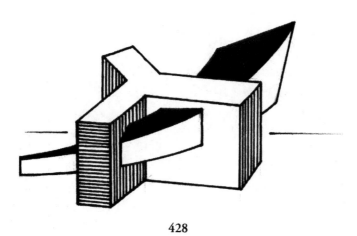

428

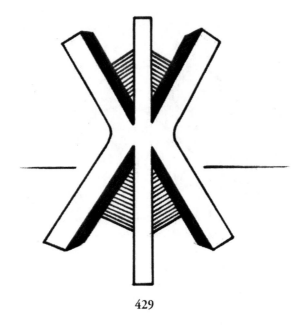

429

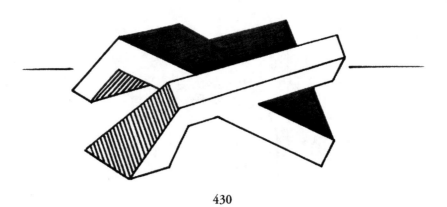

430

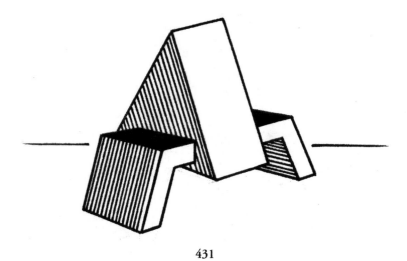

431

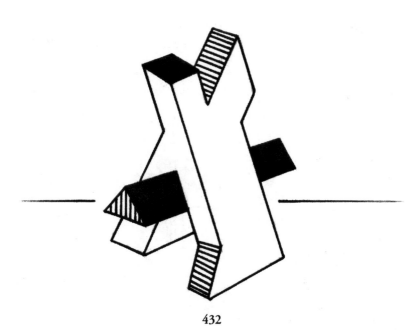

432

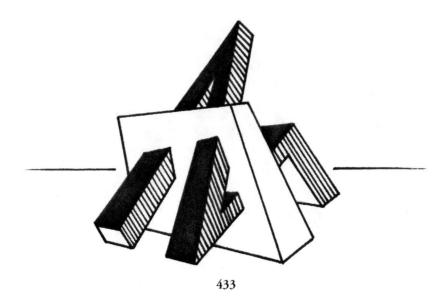

433

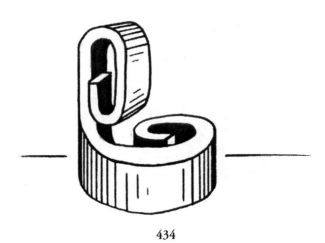

434

435

436

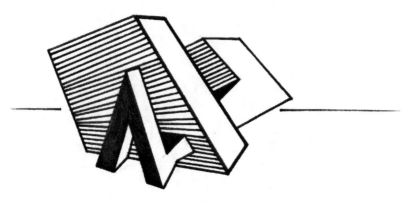

437

438

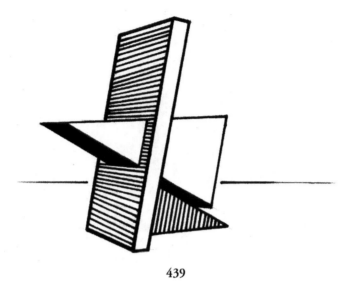

439

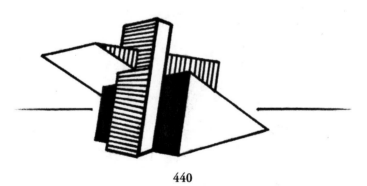

440

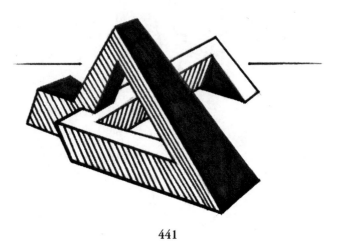

441

442

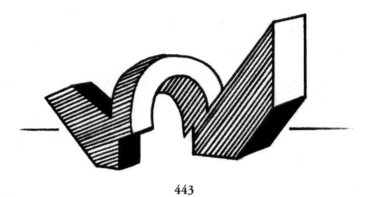

443

444

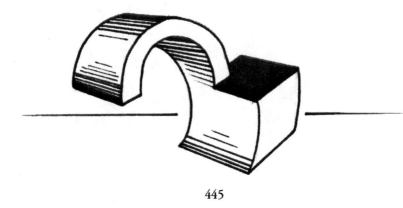

445

446

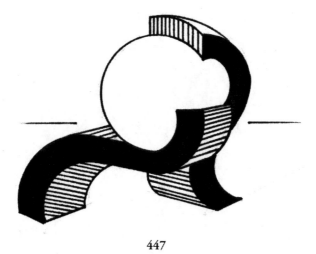

447

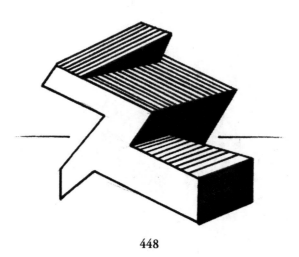

448

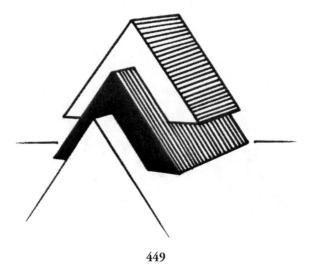

449

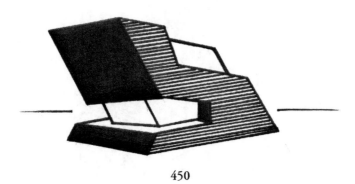

450

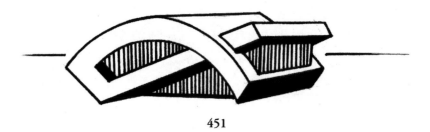

451

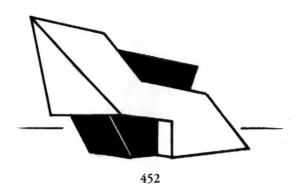

452

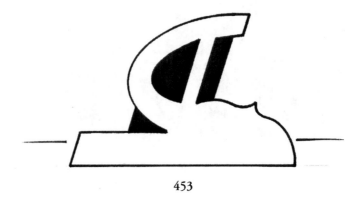

453

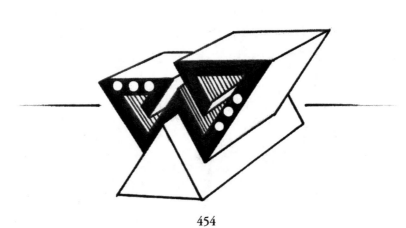

454

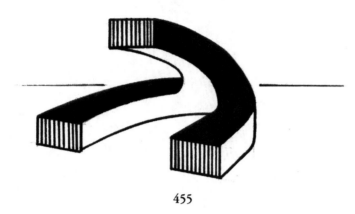

455

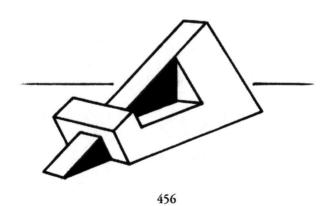

456

457

458

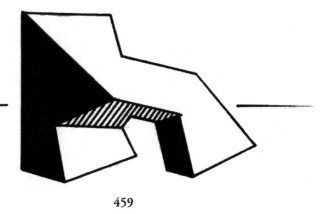

459

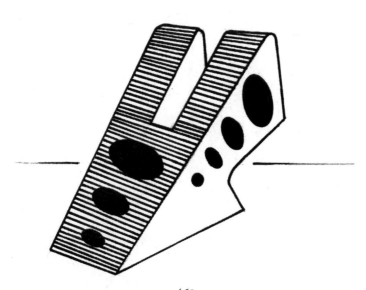

460

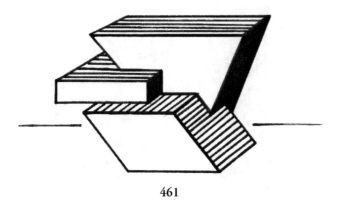

461

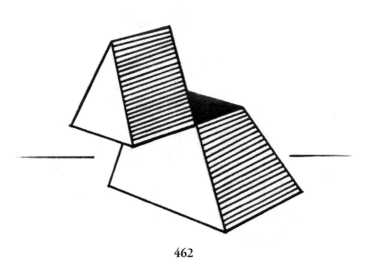

462

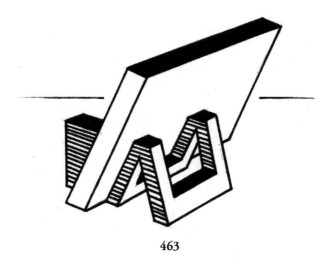

463

464

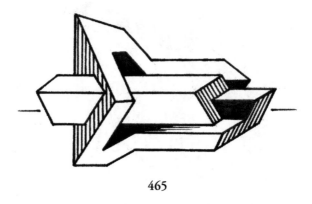

465

466

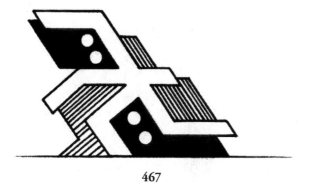

467

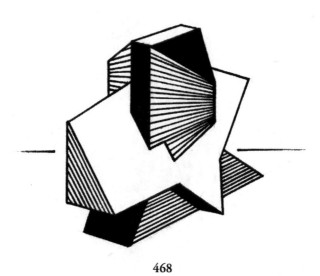

468

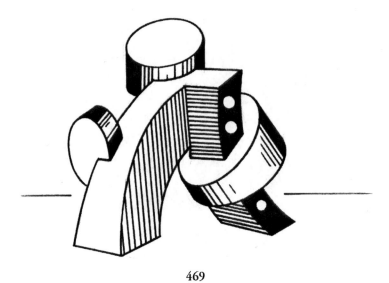

469

470

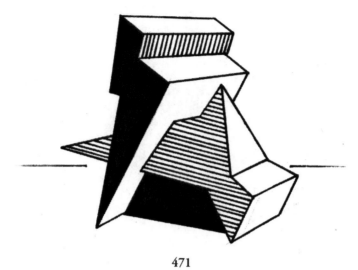

471

472

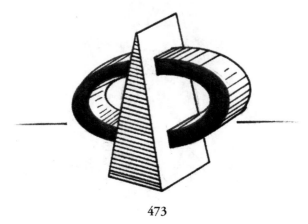

473

474

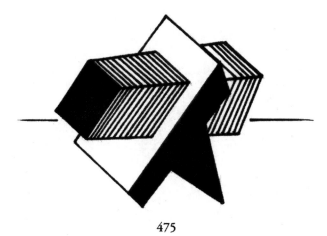

475

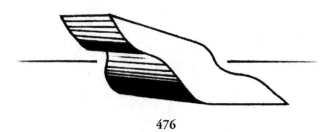

476

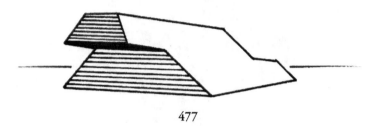

477

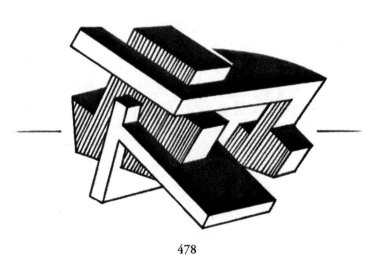

478

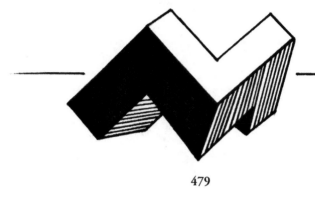

479

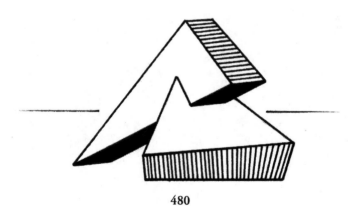

480

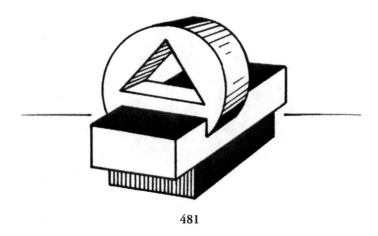

481

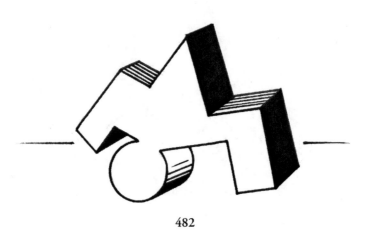

482

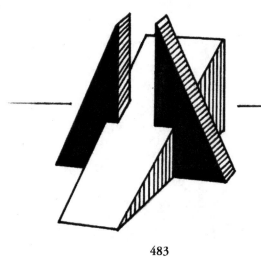

483

484

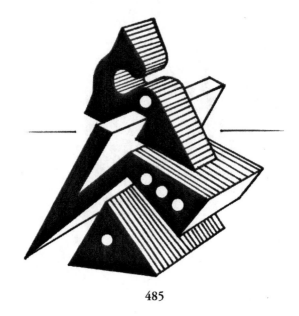

485

486

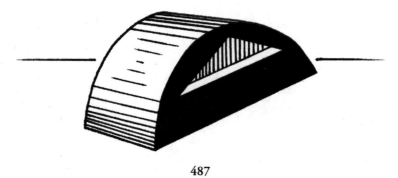

487

488

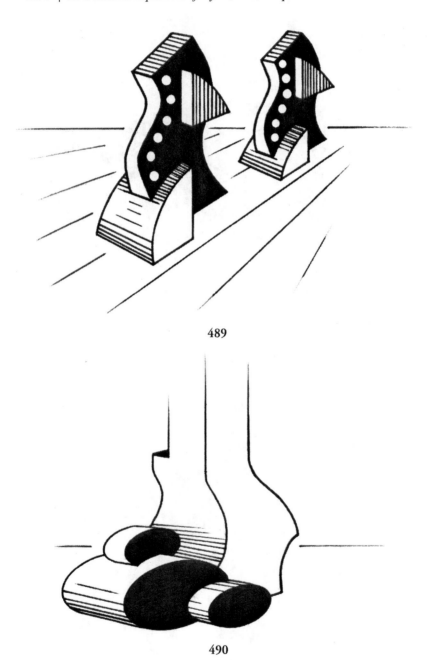

489

490

491

492

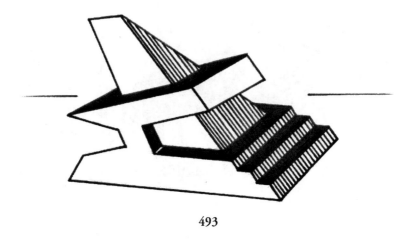

493

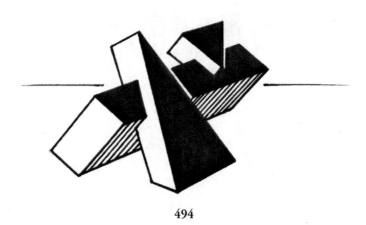

494

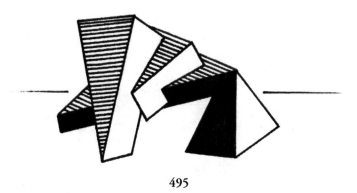

495

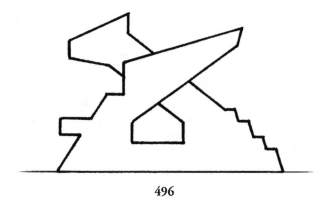

496

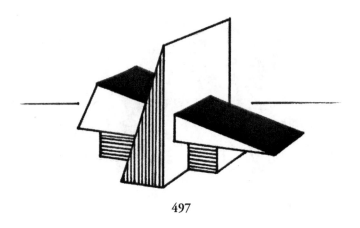

497

498

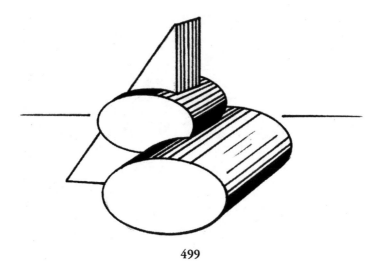

499

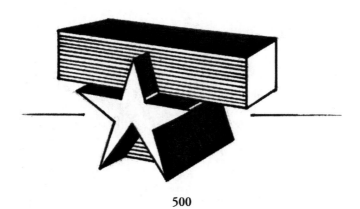

500

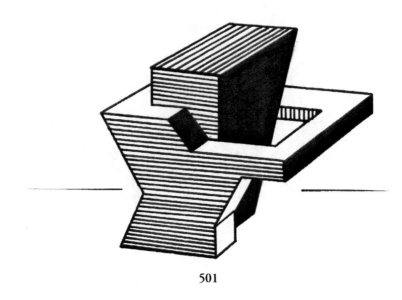

501

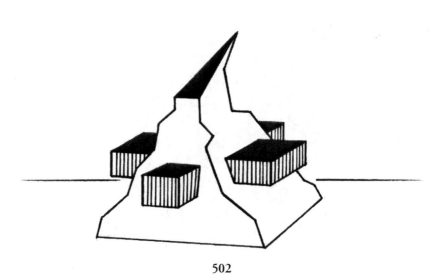

502

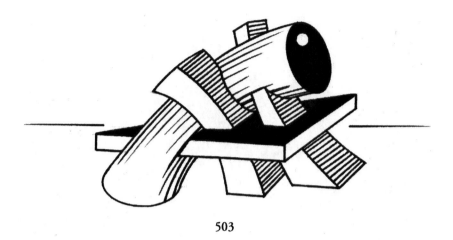

503

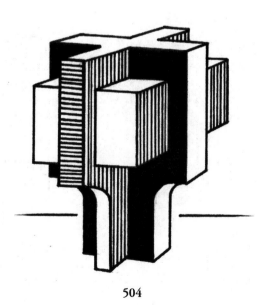

504

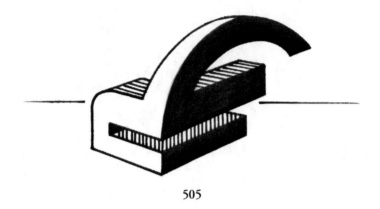

505

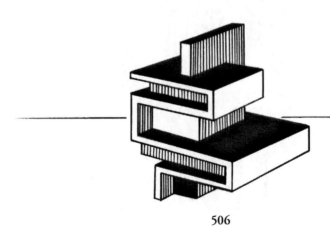

506

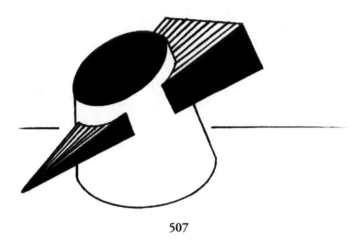

507

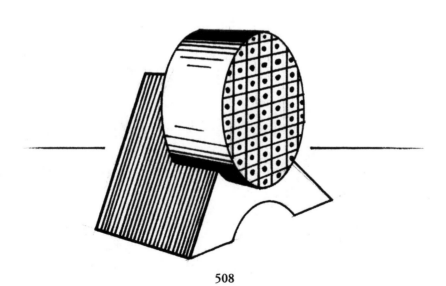

508

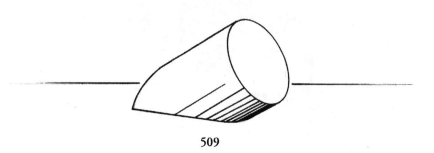

509

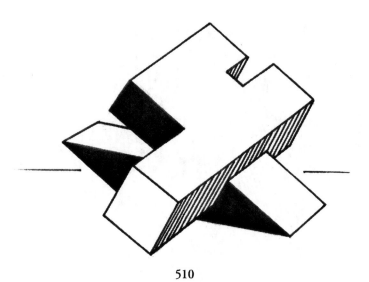

510

511

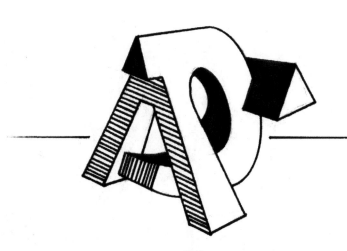

512

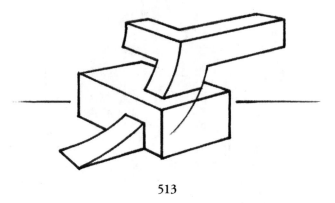

513

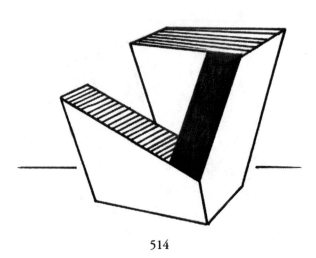

514

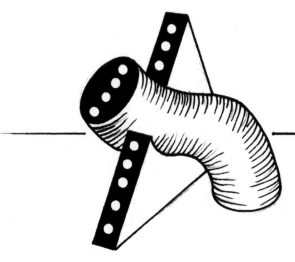

515

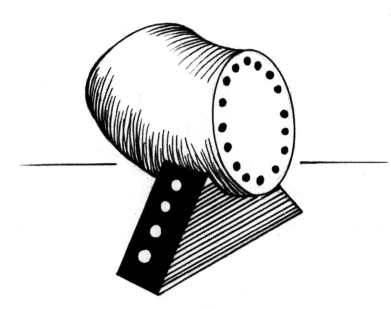

516

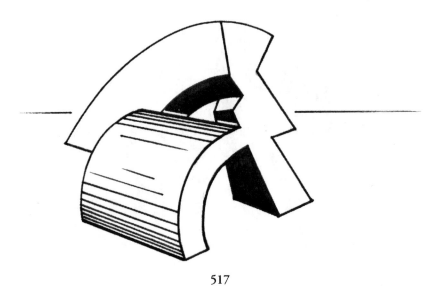

517

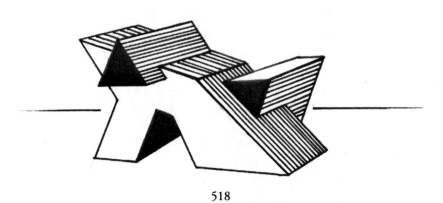

518

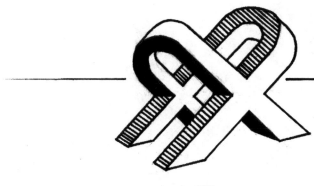

519

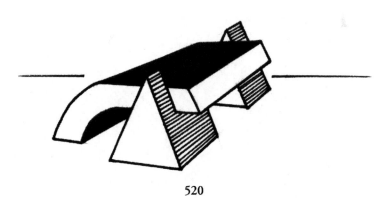

520

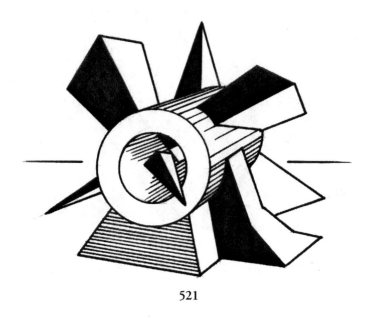

521

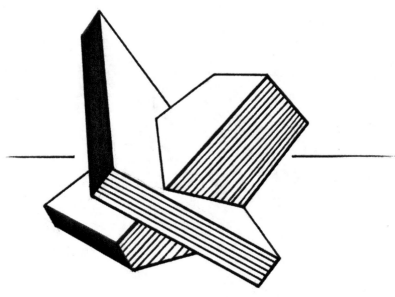

522

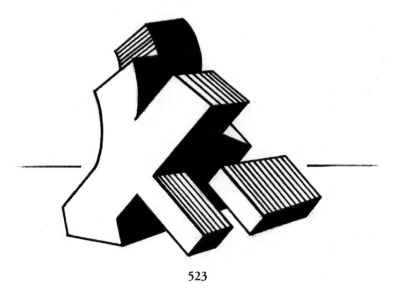

523

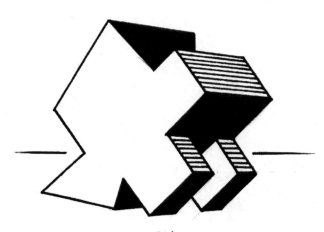

524

525

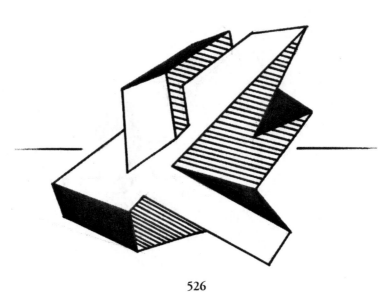

526

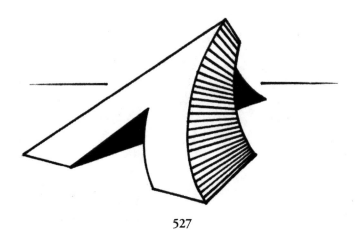

527

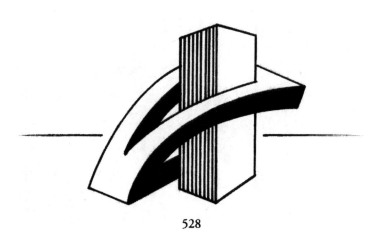

528

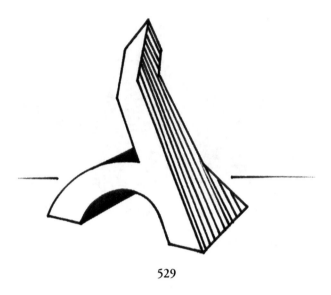

529

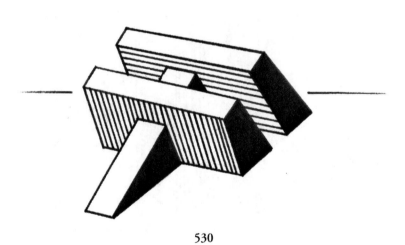

530

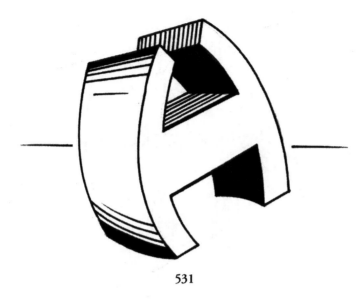

531

532

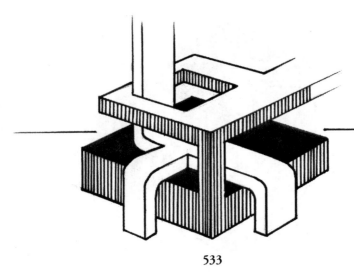

533

534

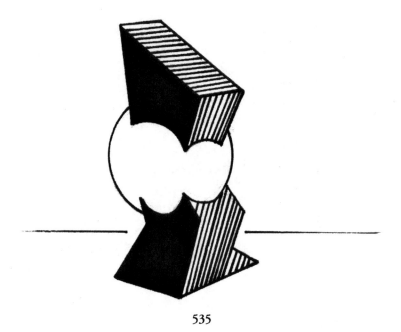

535

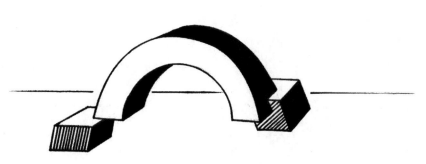

536

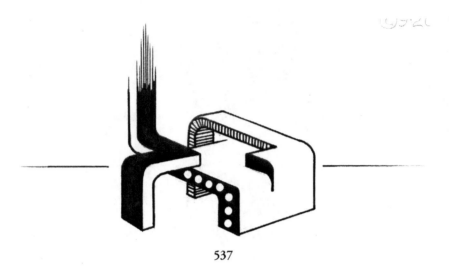

537

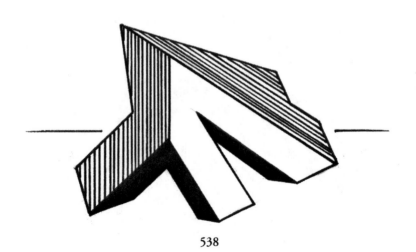

538

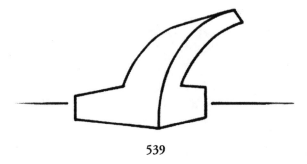

539

540

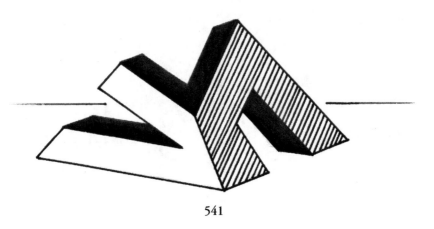

541

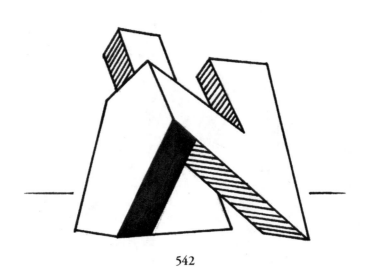

542

543

544

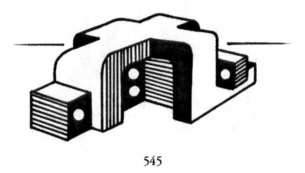

545

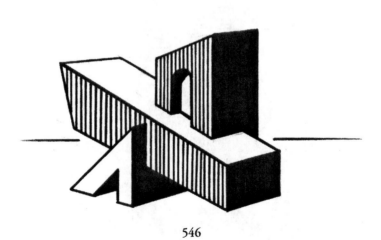

546

547

548

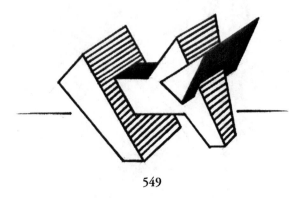

549

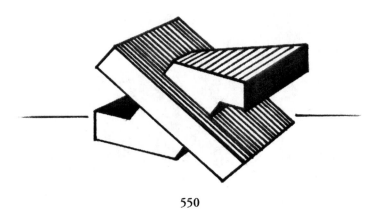

550

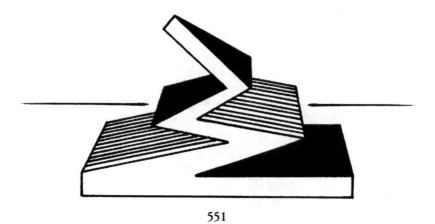

551

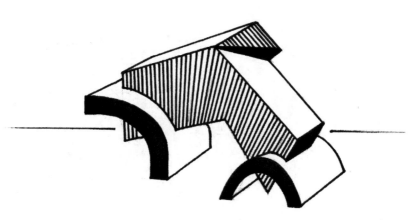

552

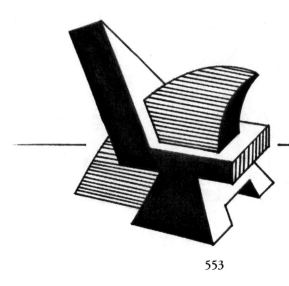

553

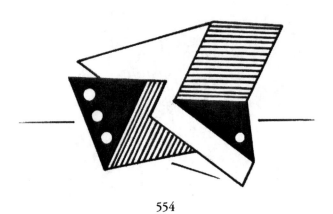

554

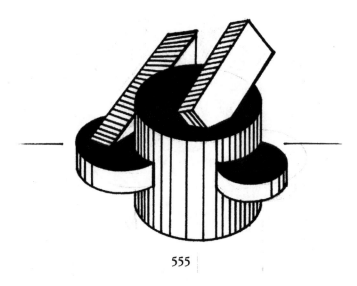

555

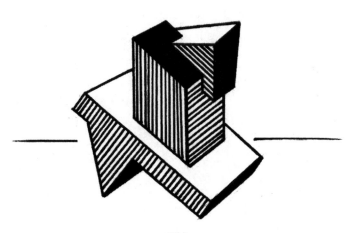

556

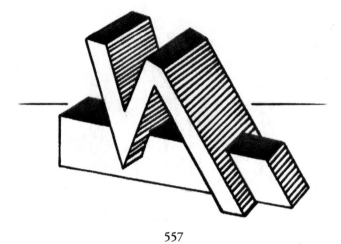

557

558

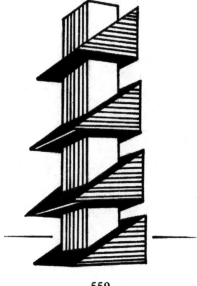

559

560

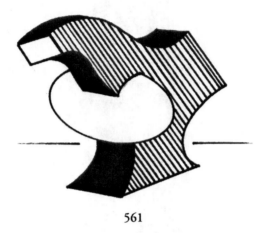

561

562

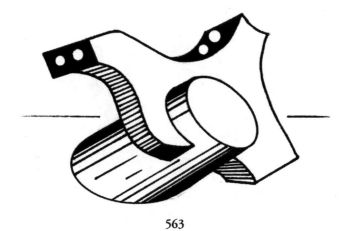

563

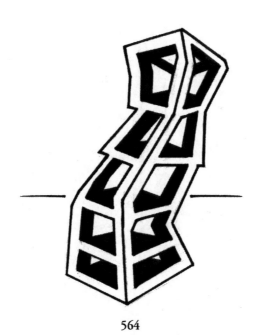

564

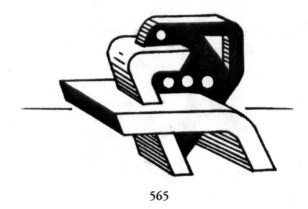

565

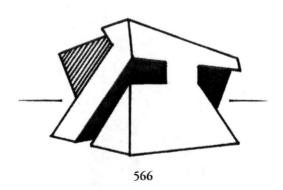

566

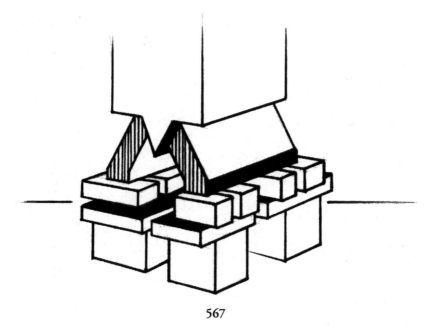

567

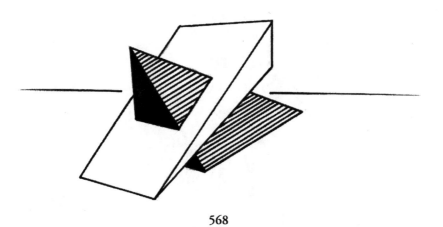

568

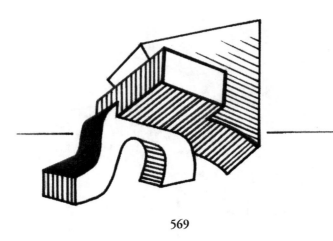

569

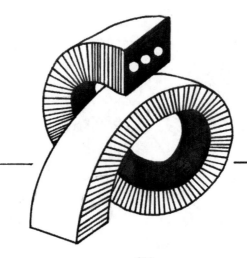

570

571

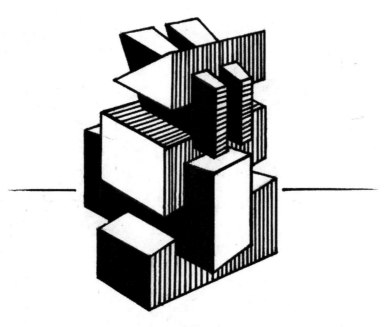

572

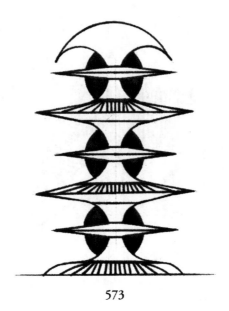

573

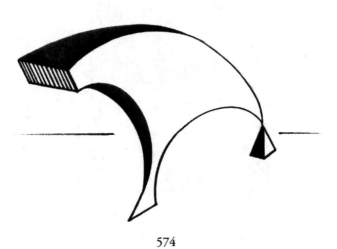

574

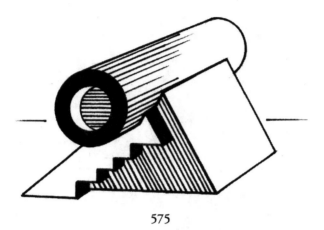

575

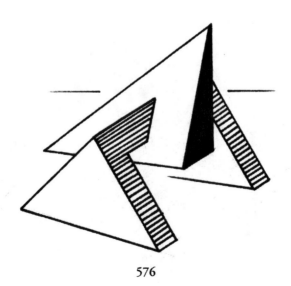

576

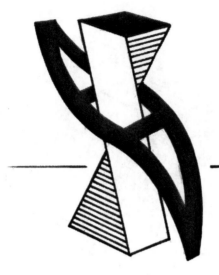

577

578

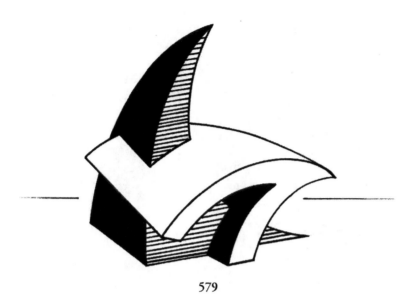

579

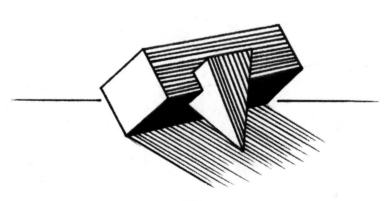

580

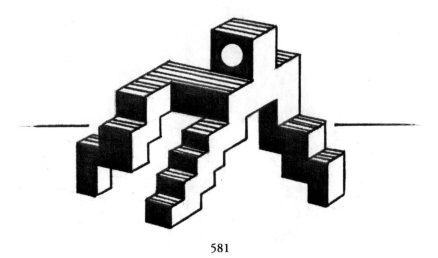

581

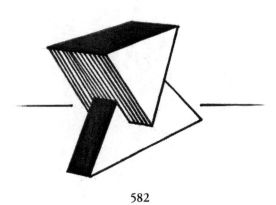

582

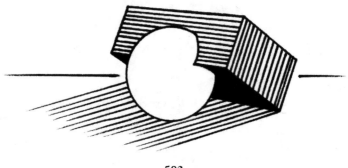

583

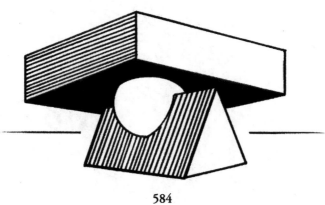

584

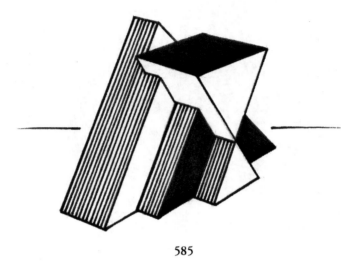

585

586

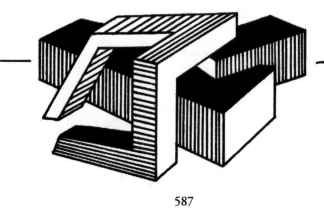

587

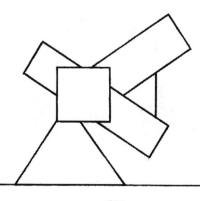

588

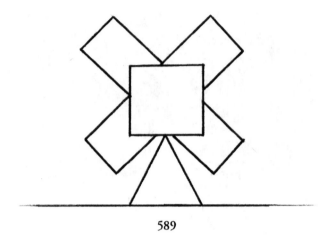

589

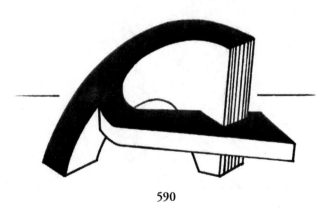

590

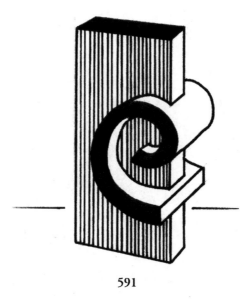

591

592

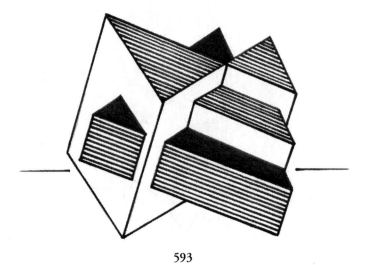

593

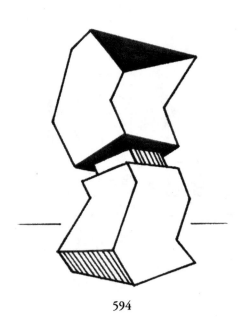

594

595

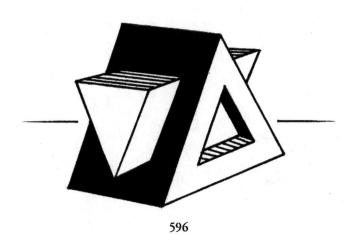

596

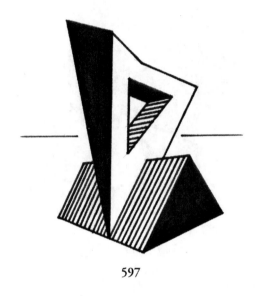

597

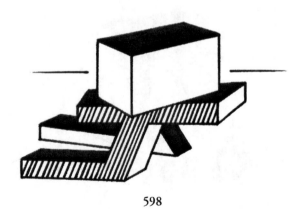

598

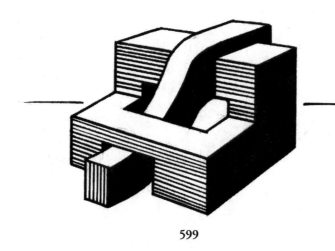

599

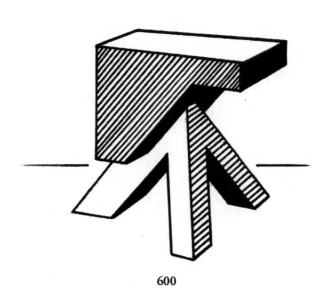

600

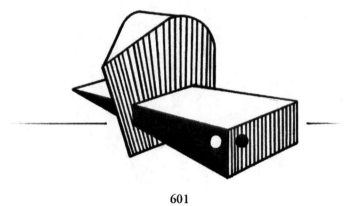

601

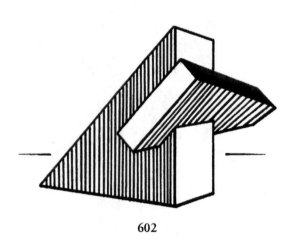

602

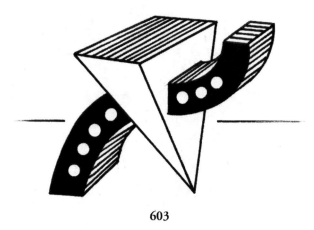

603

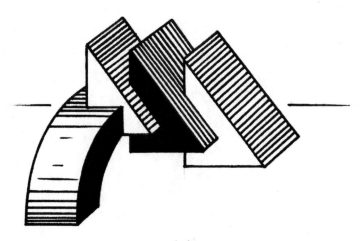

604

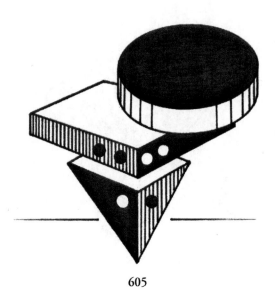

605

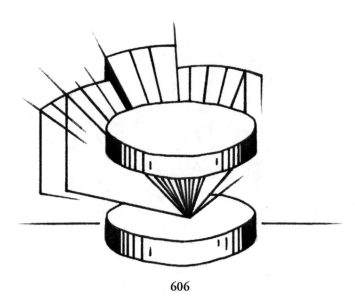

606

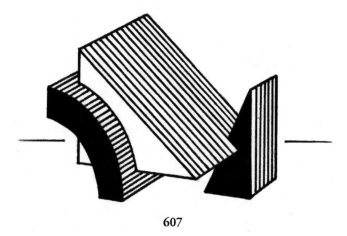

607

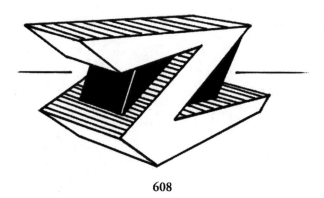

608

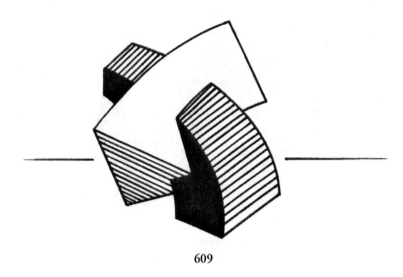

609

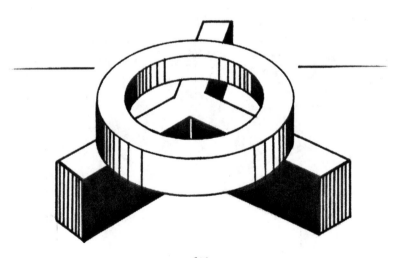

610

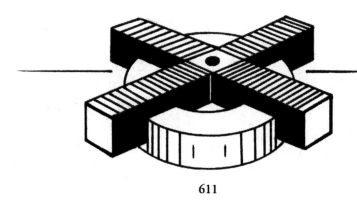

611

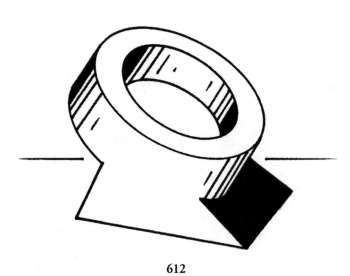

612

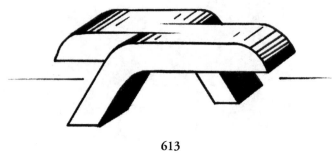

613

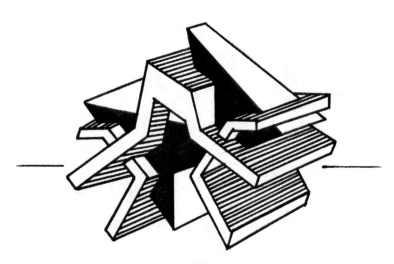

614

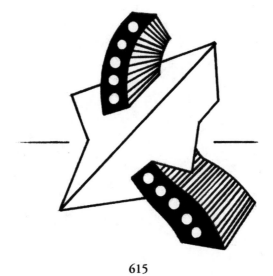

615

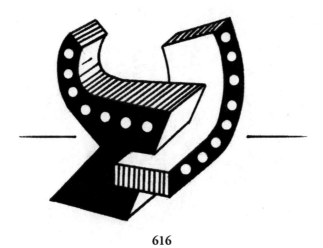

616

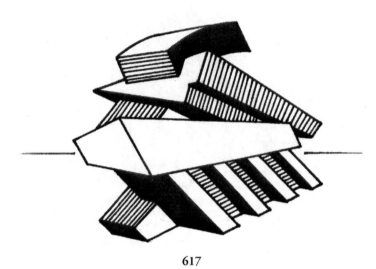

617

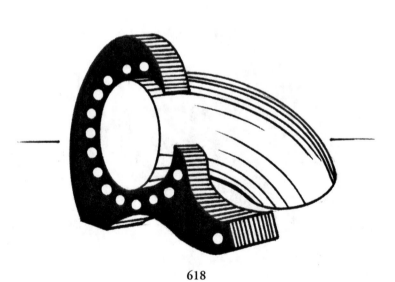

618

619

620

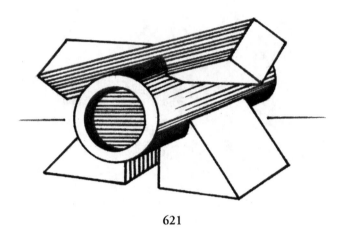

621

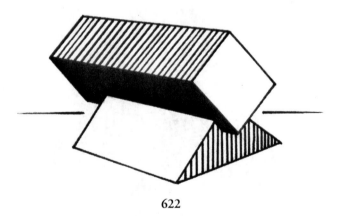

622

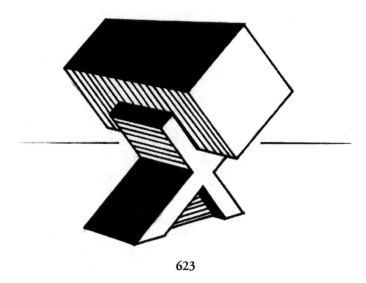

623

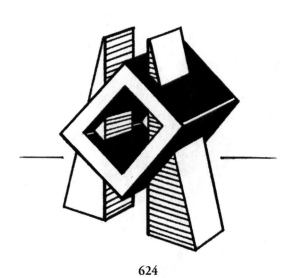

624

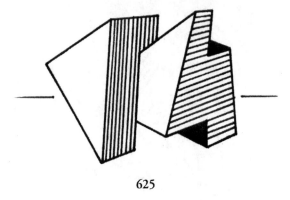

625

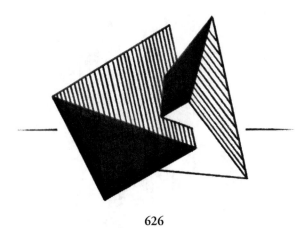

626

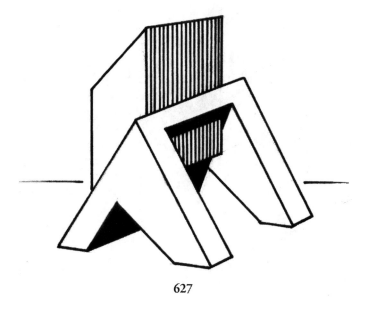

627

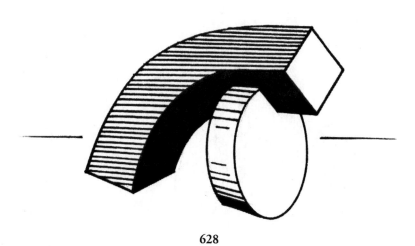

628

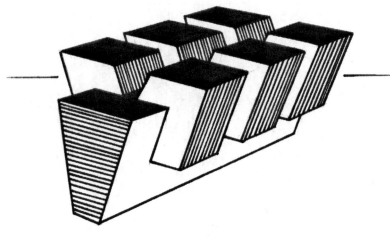

629

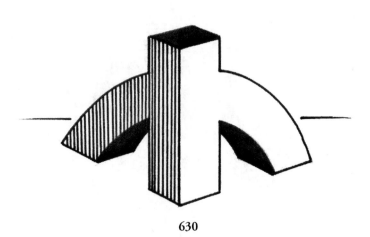

630

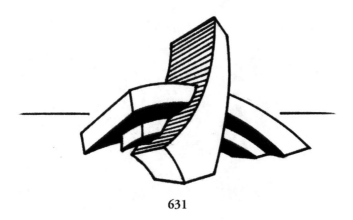

631

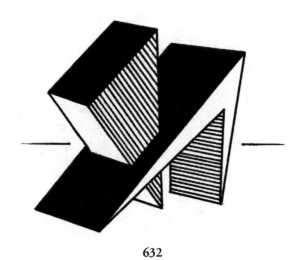

632

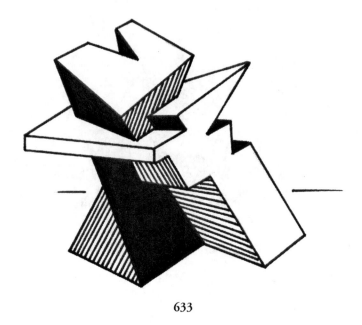

633

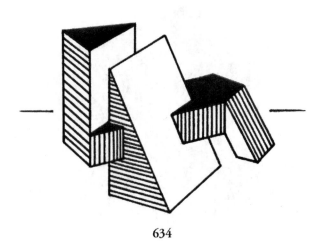

634

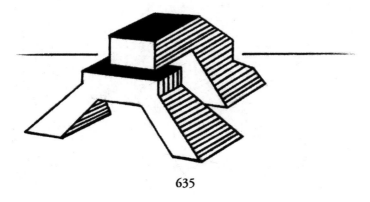

635

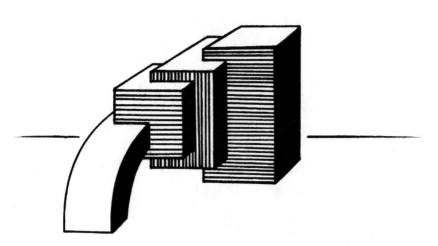

636

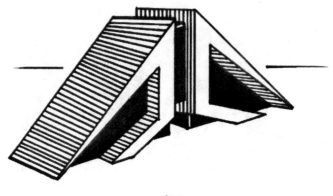

637

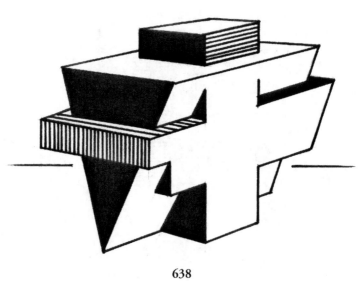

638

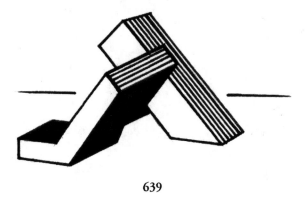

639

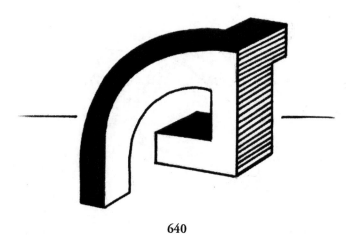

640

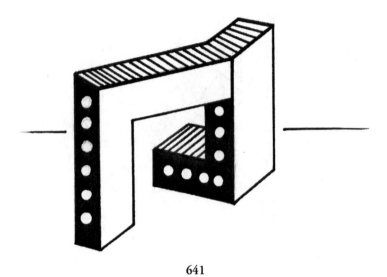

641

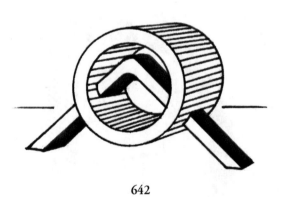

642

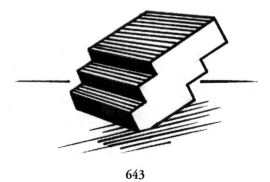

643

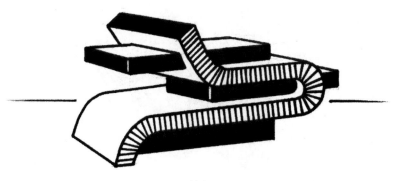

644

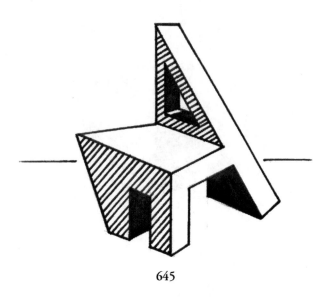

645

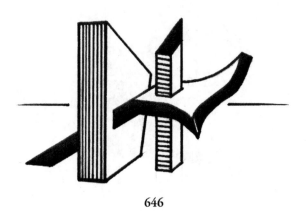

646

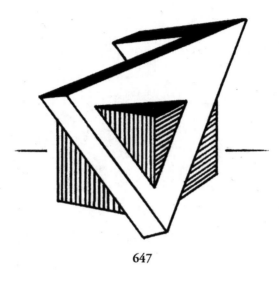

647

648

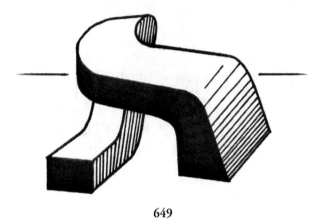

649

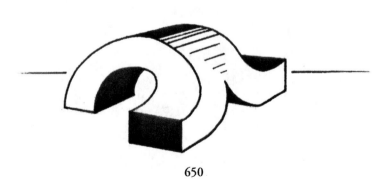

650

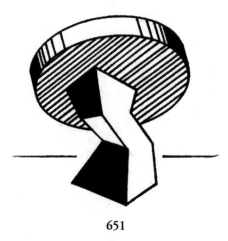

651

652

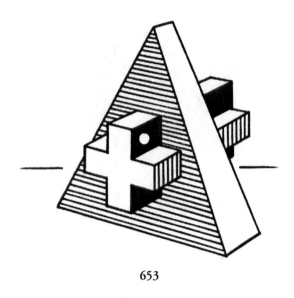

653

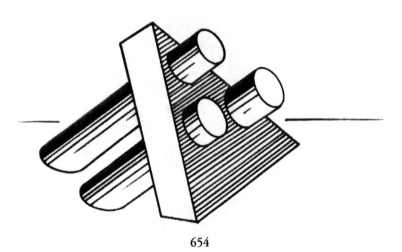

654

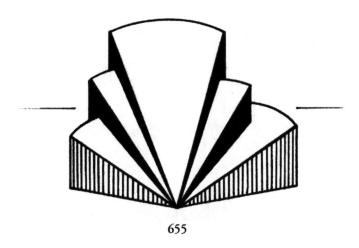

655

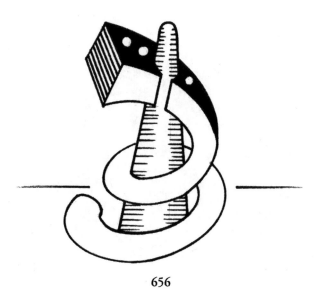

656

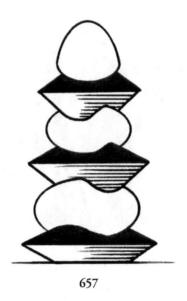

657

658

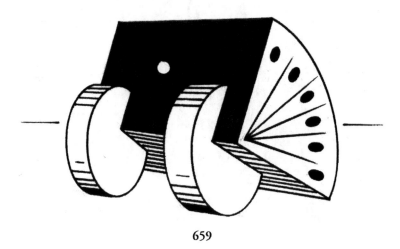

659

660

661

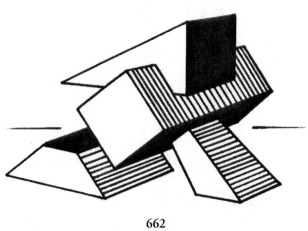

662

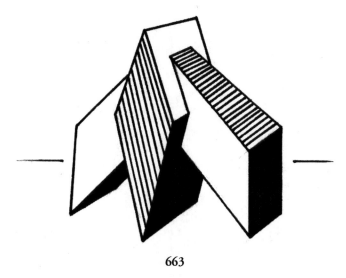

663

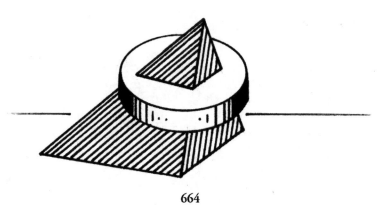

664

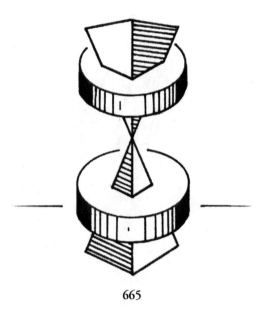

665

666

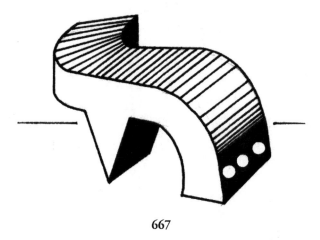

667

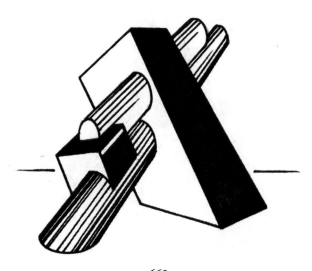

668

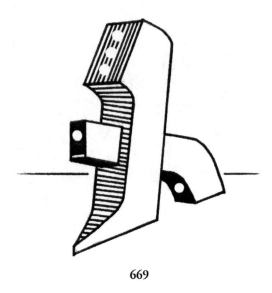

669

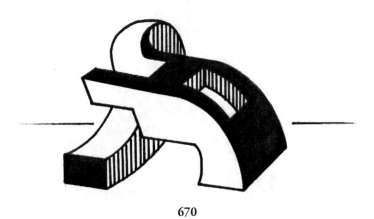

670

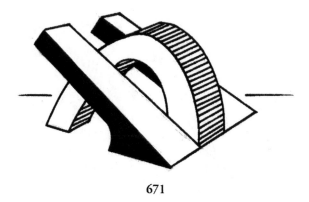

671

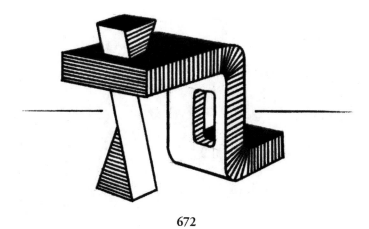

672

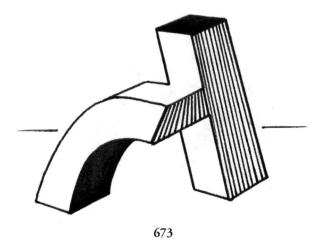

673

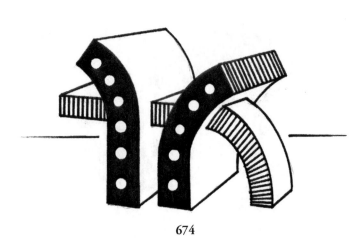

674

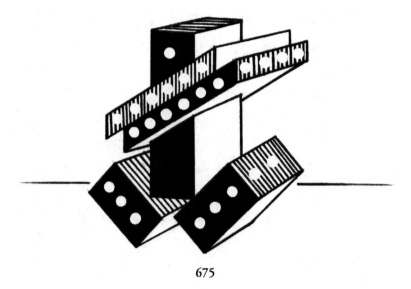

675

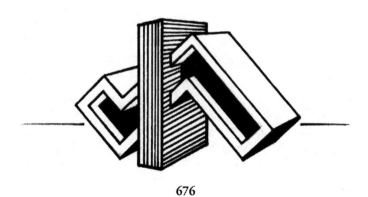

676

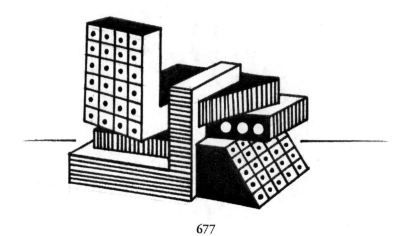

677

678

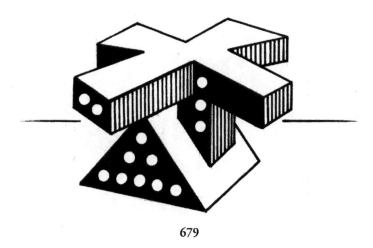

679

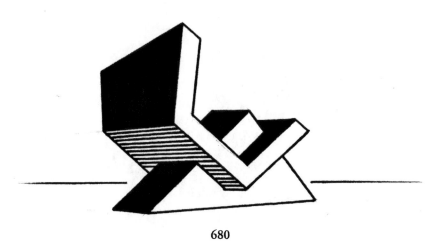

680

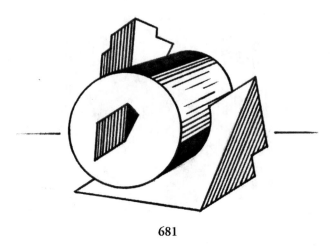

681

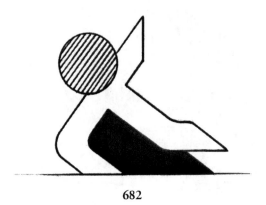

682

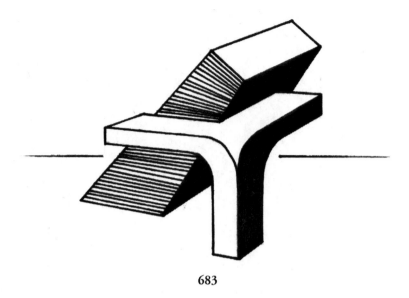

683

684

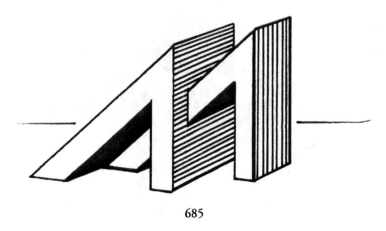

685

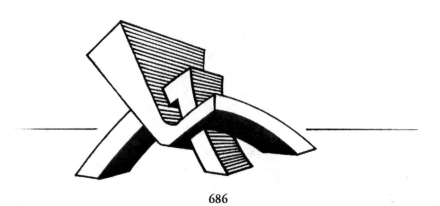

686

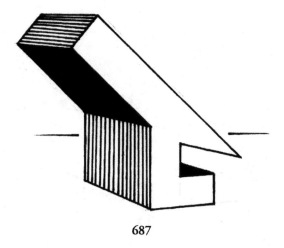

687

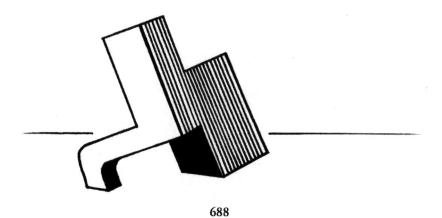

688

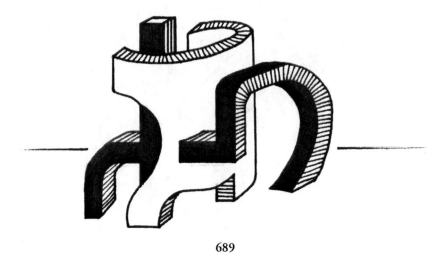

689

690

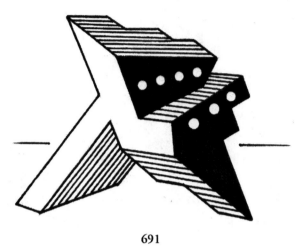

691

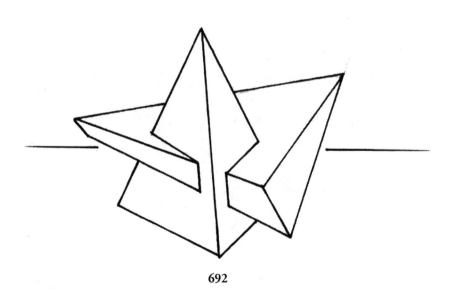

692

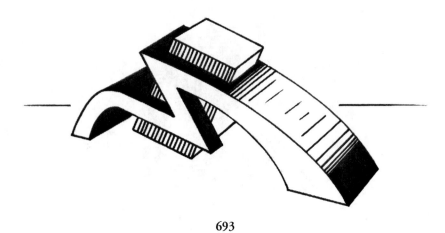

693

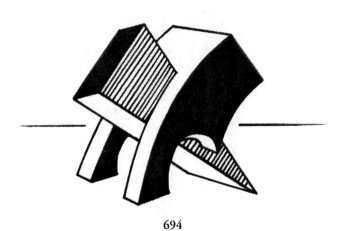

694

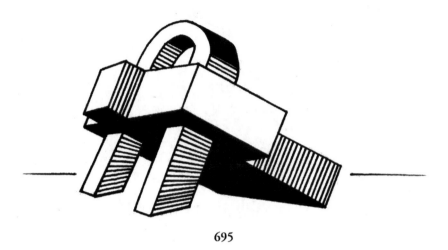

695

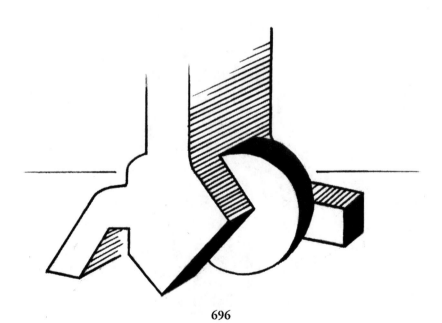

696

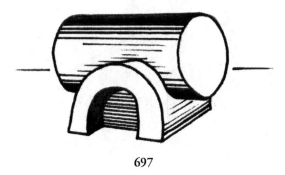

697

698

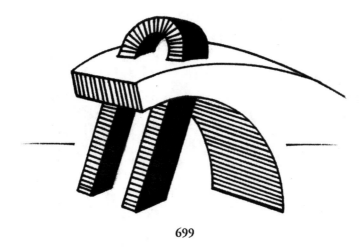

699

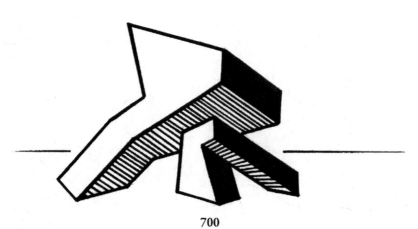

700

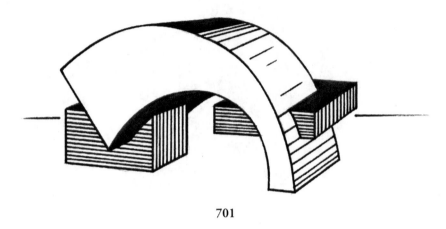

701

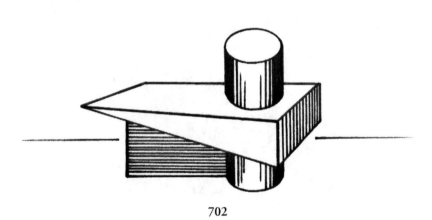

702

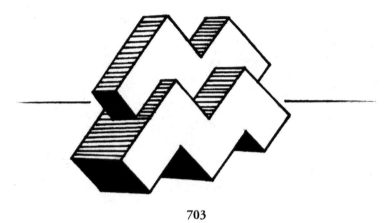

703

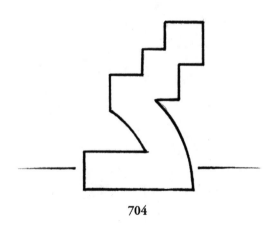

704

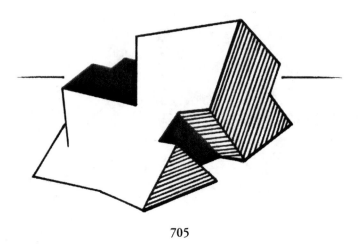

705

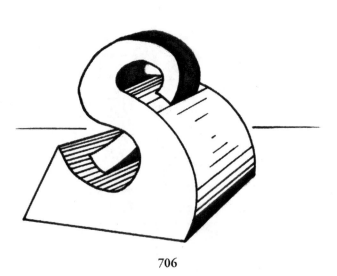

706

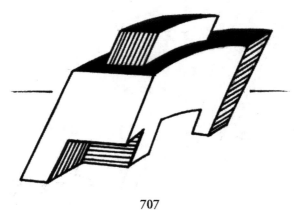

707

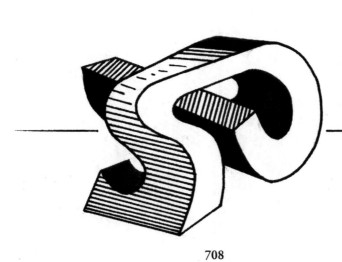

708

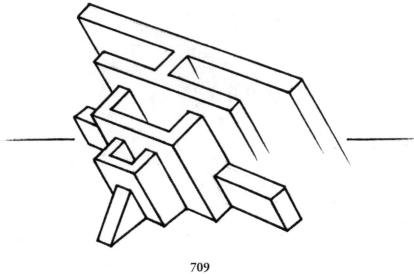

709

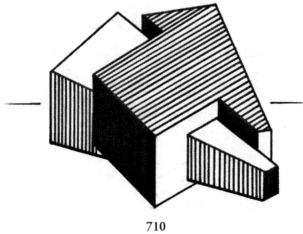

710

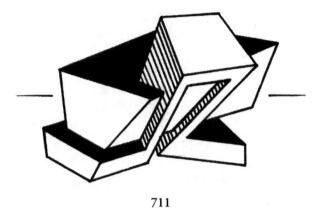

711

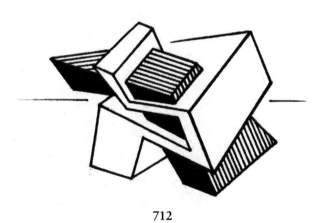

712

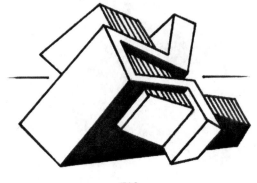

713

714

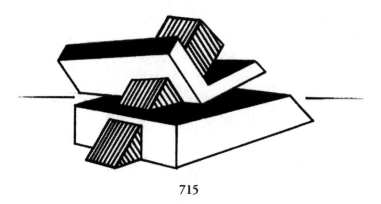

715

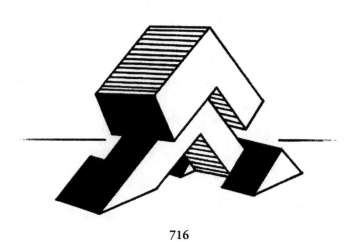

716

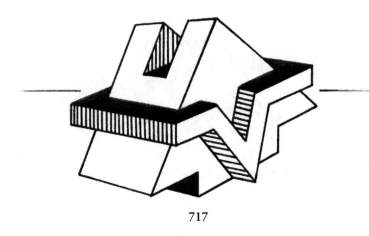

717

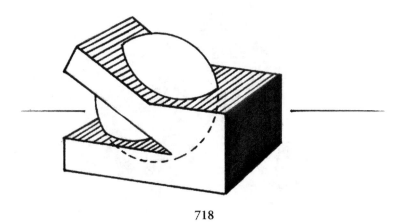

718

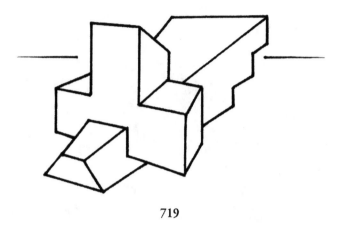

719

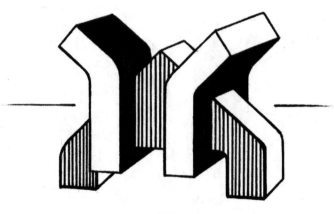

720

721

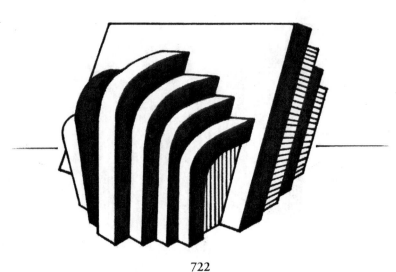

722

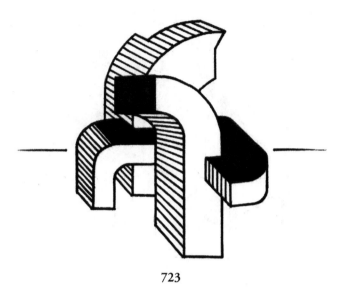

723

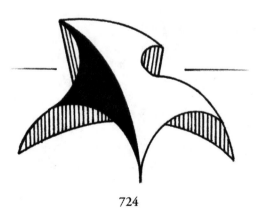

724

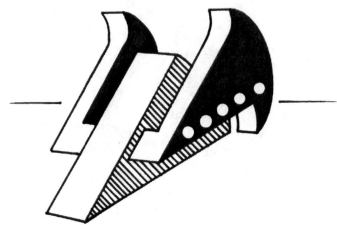

725

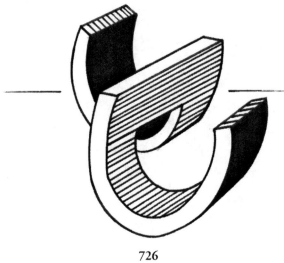

726

727

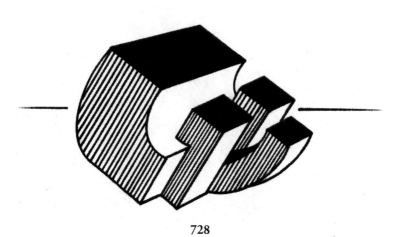

728

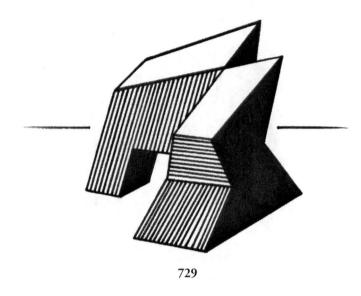

729

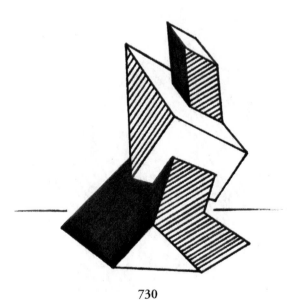

730

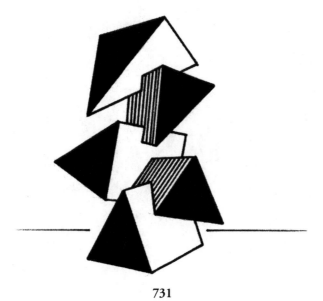

731

732

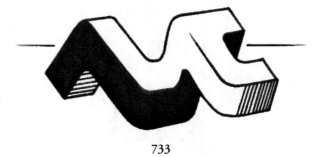

733

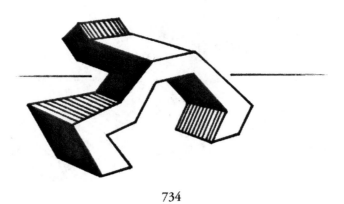

734

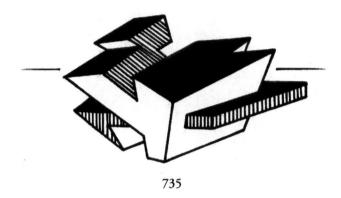

735

736

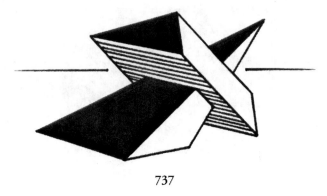

737

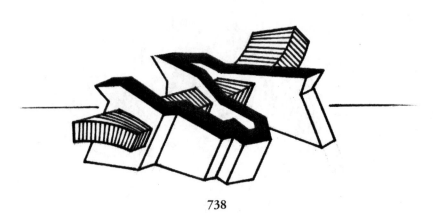

738

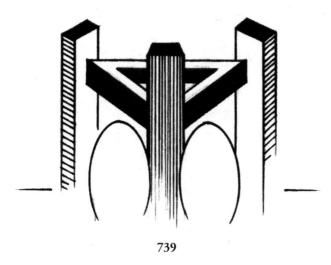

739

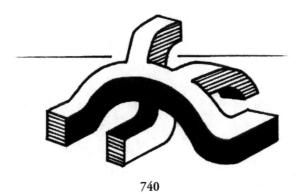

740

741

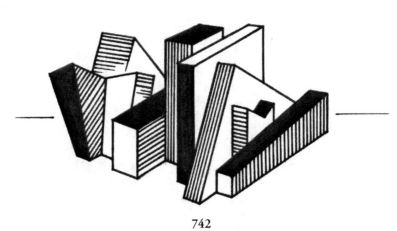

742

743

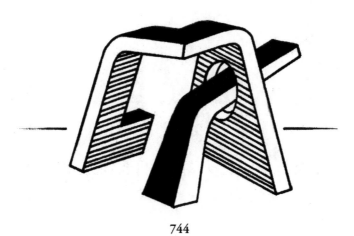

744

745

746

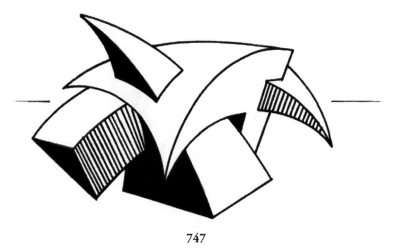

747

748

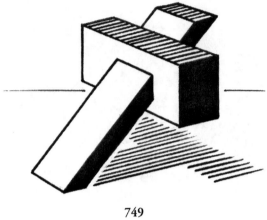

749

750

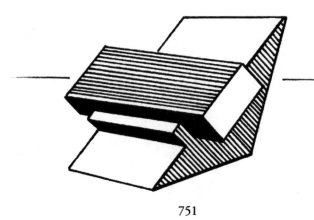

751

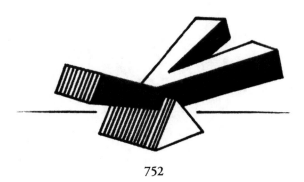

752

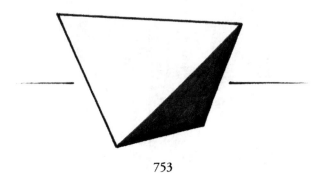

753

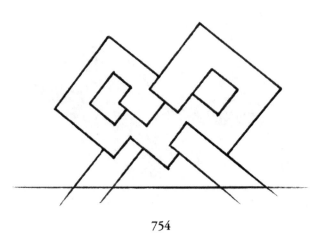

754

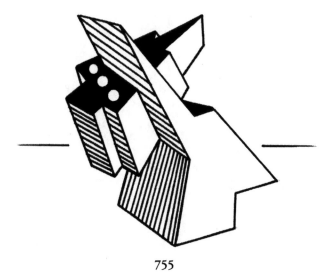

755

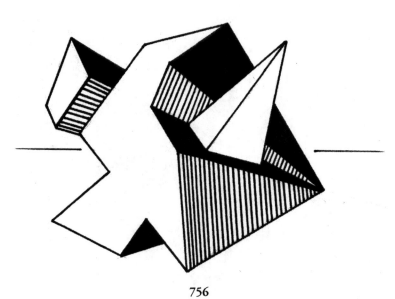

756

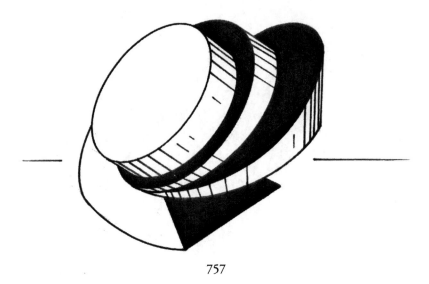

757

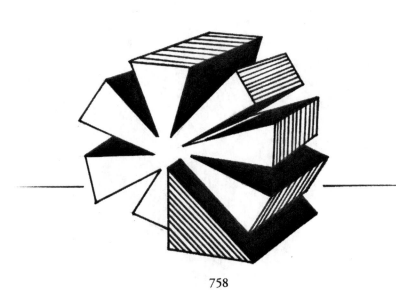

758

759

760

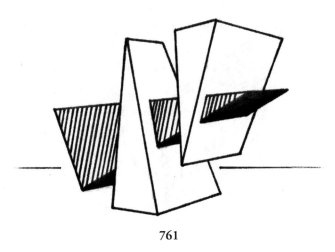

761

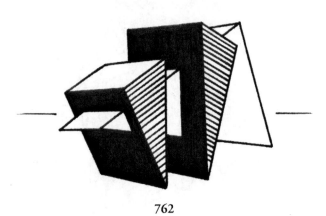

762

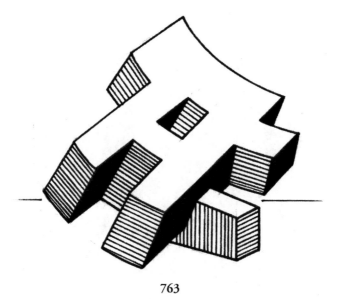

763

764

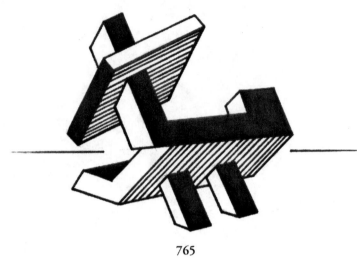

765

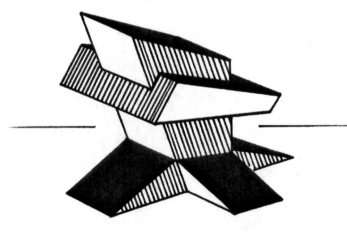

766

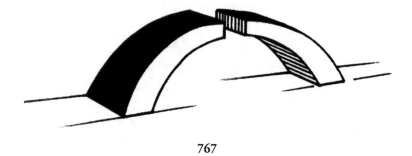

767

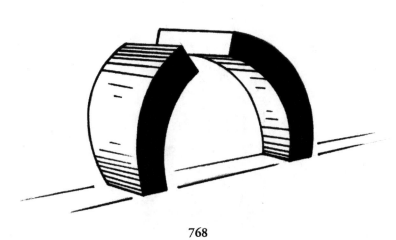

768

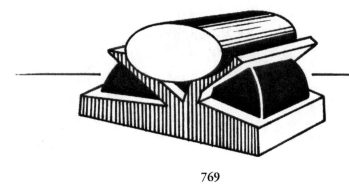

769

770

771

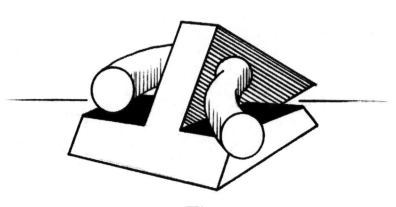

772

773

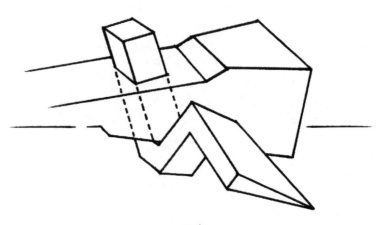

774

775

776

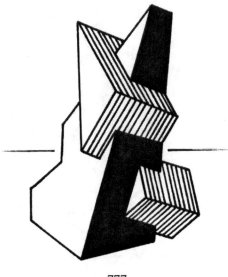

777

778

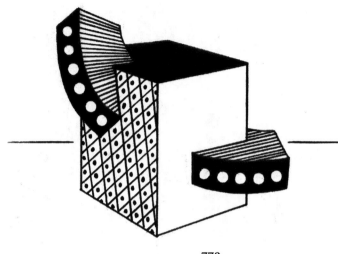

779

780

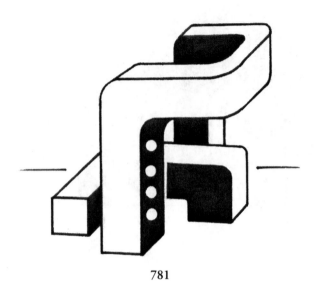

781

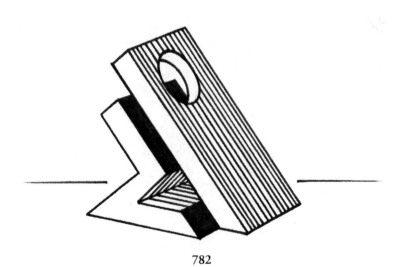

782

783

784

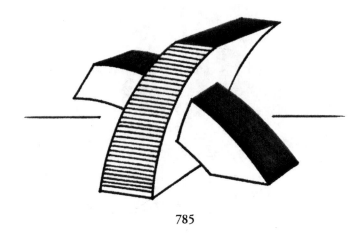

785

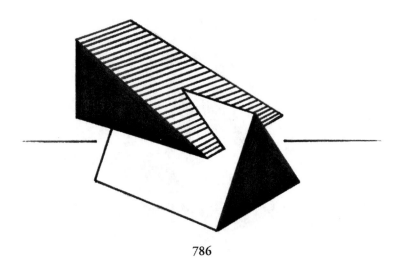

786

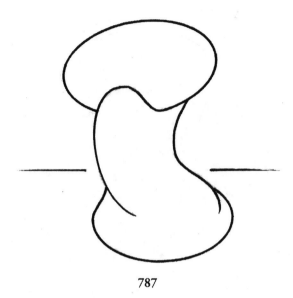

787

788

789

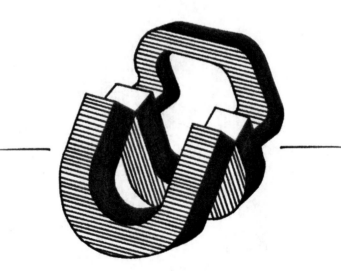

790

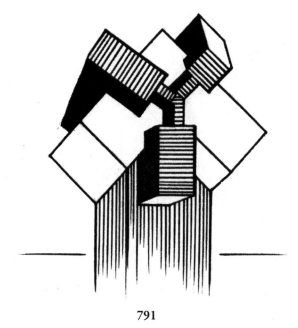

791

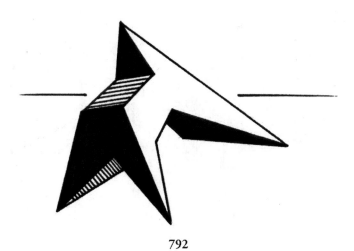

792

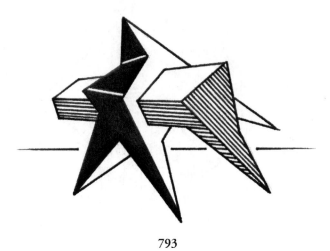

793

794

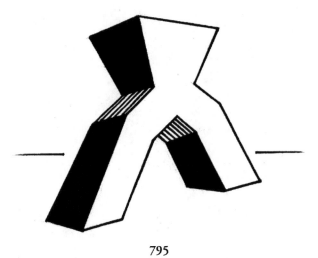

795

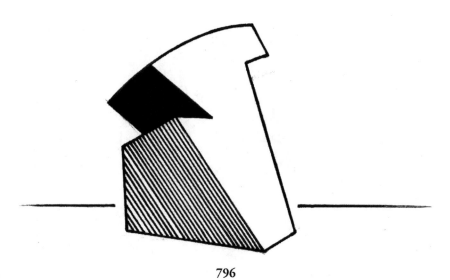

796

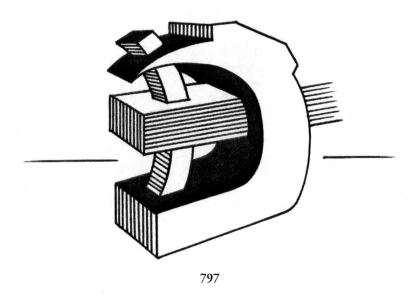

797

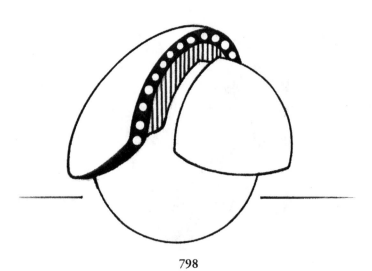

798

799

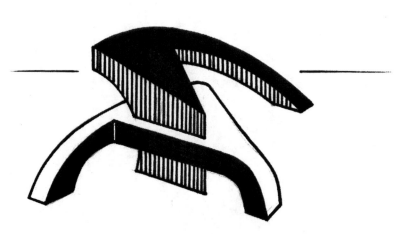

800

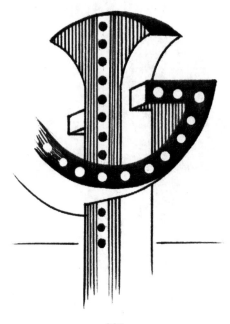

801

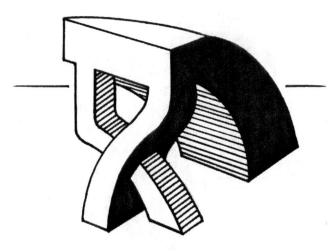

802

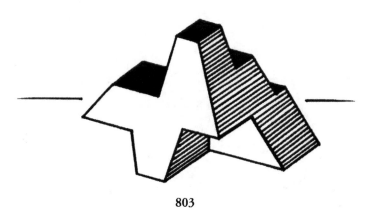

803

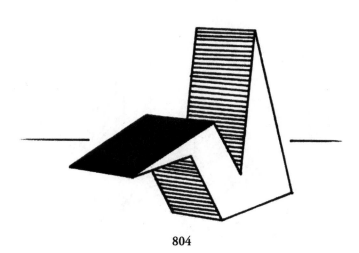

804

805

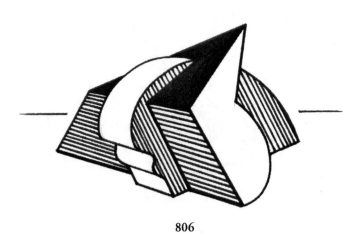

806

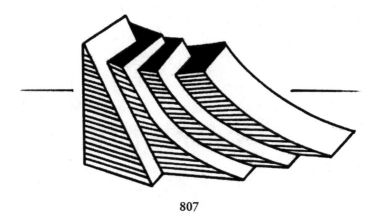

807

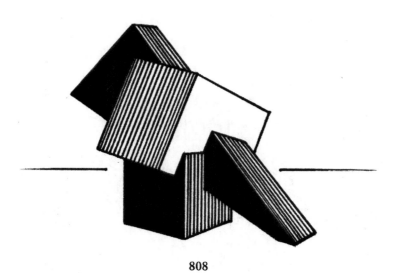

808

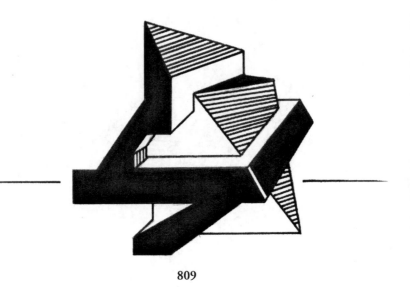

809

810

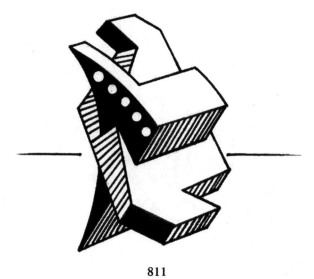

811

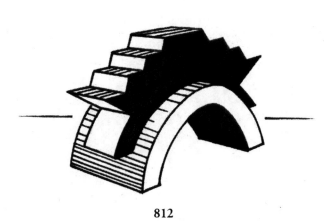

812

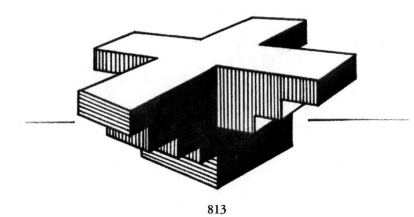

813

814

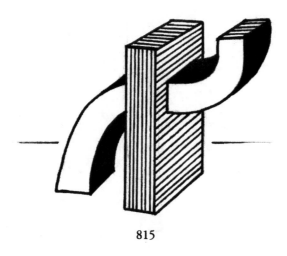

815

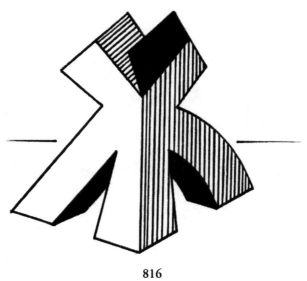

816

817

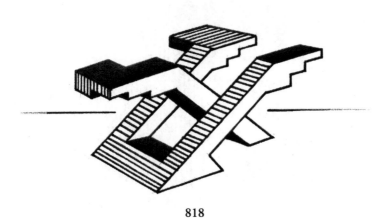

818

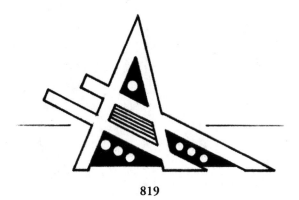

819

820

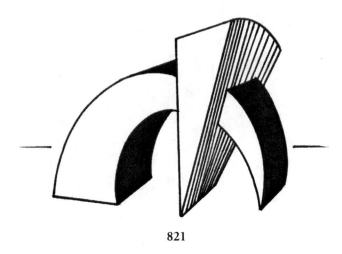

821

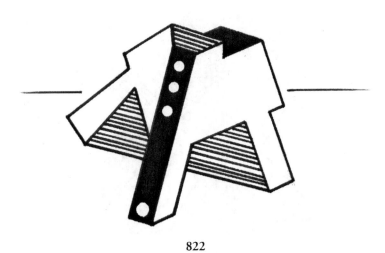

822

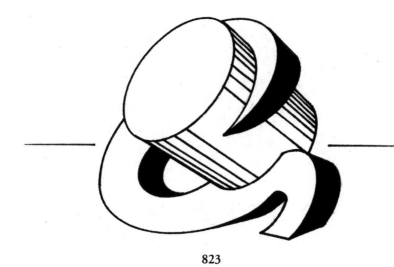

823

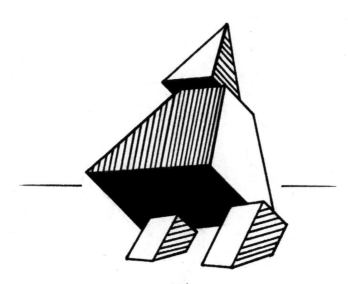

824

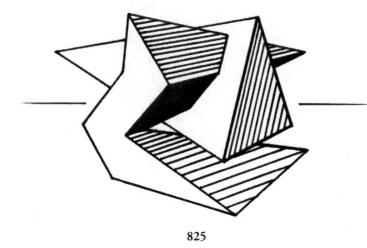

825

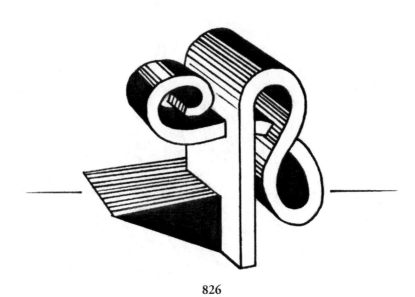

826

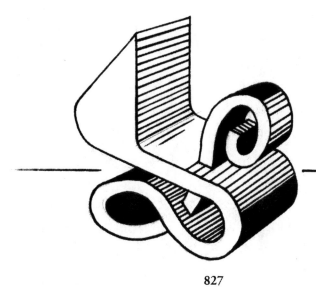

827

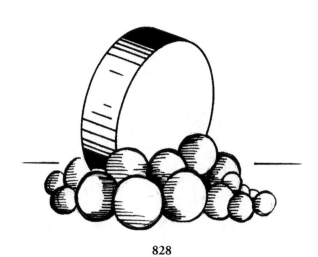

828

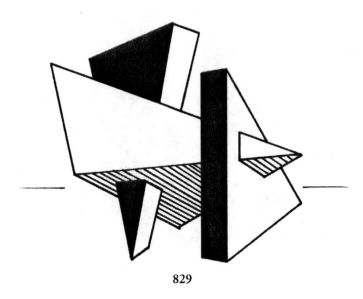

829

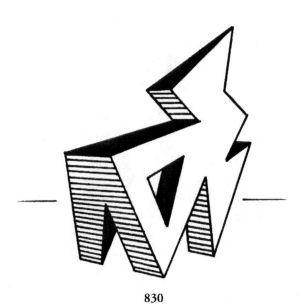

830

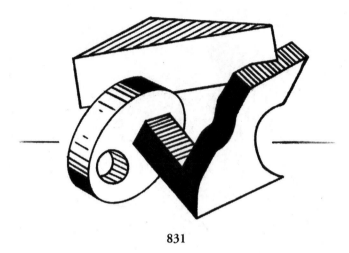

831

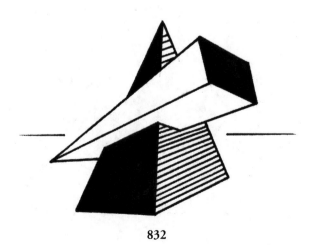

832

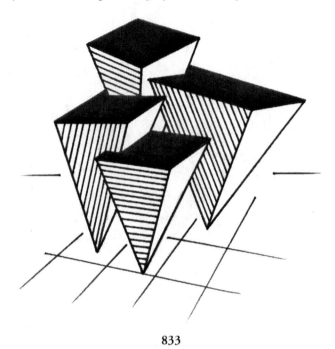

833

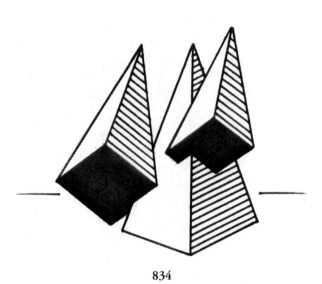

834

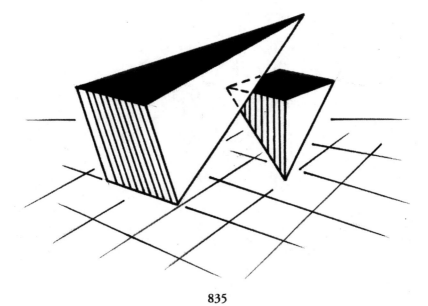

835

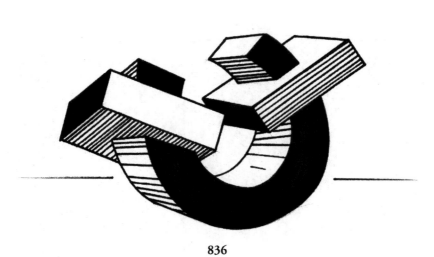

836

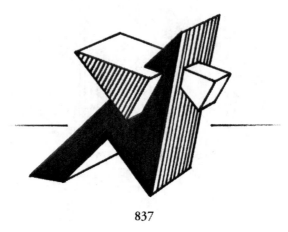

837

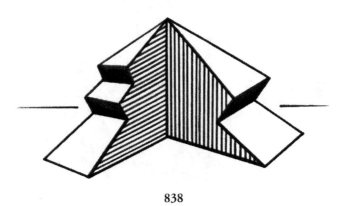

838

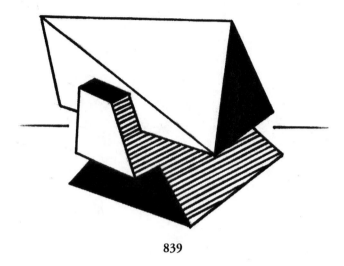

839

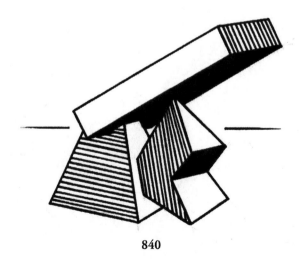

840

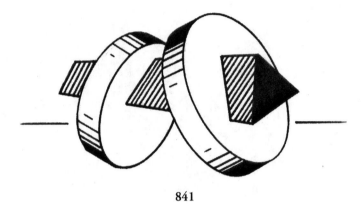

841

842

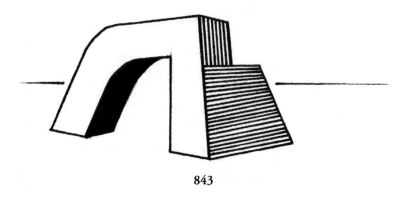

843

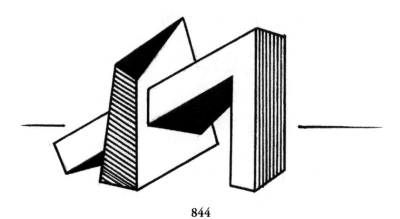

844

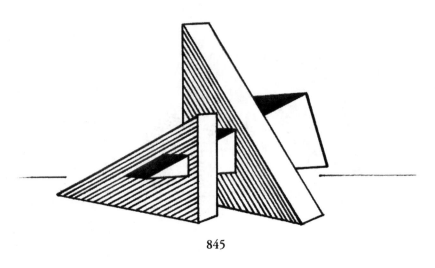

845

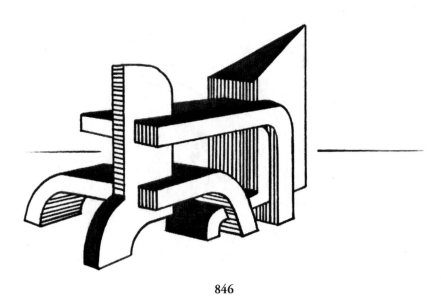

846

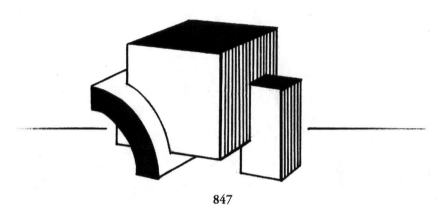

847

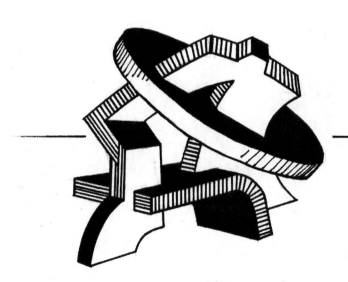

848

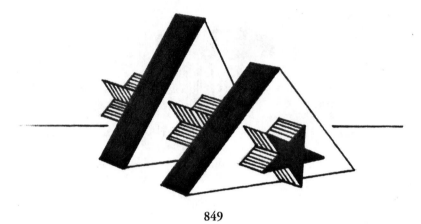

849

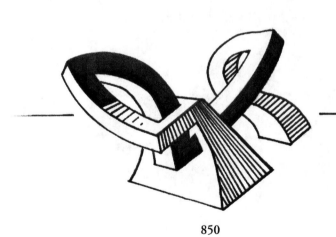

850

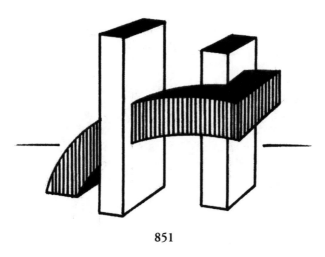

851

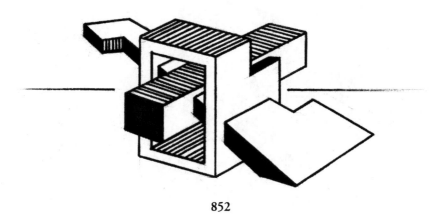

852

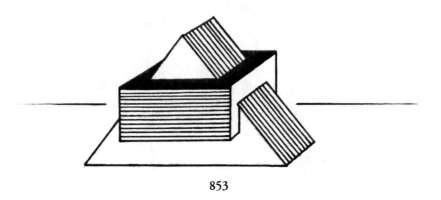

853

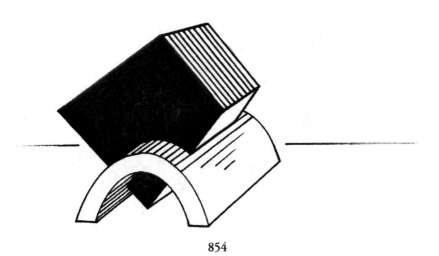

854

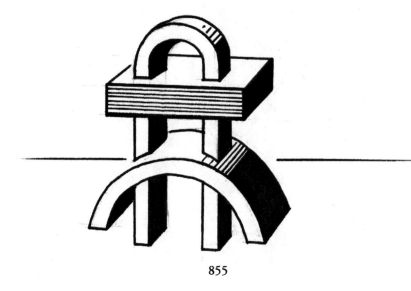

855

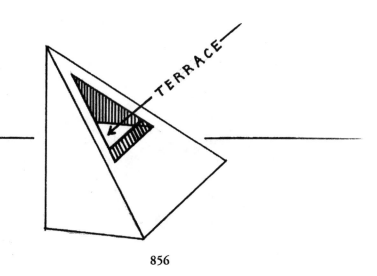

856

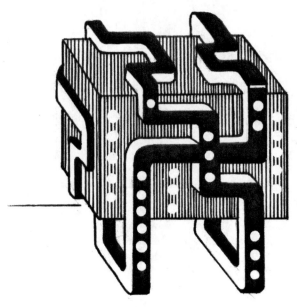

857

858

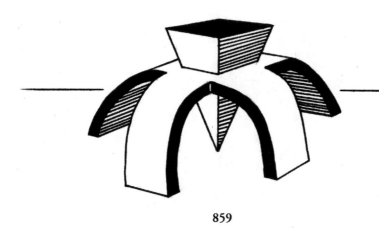

859

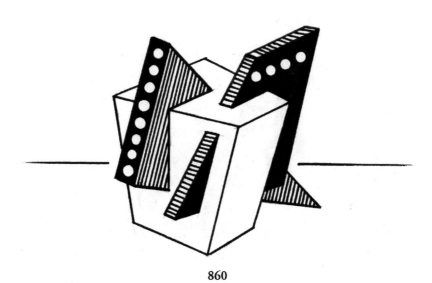

860

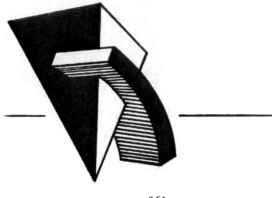

861

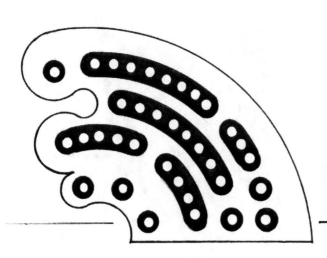

862

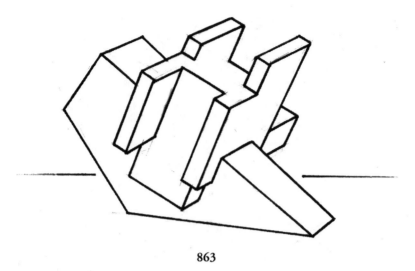

863

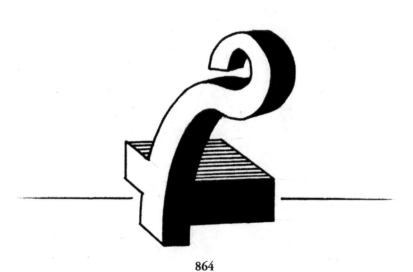

864

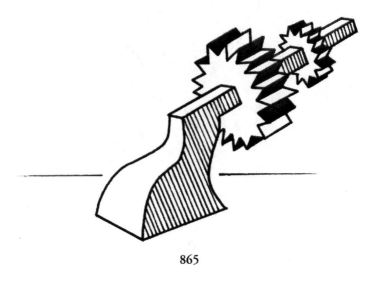

865

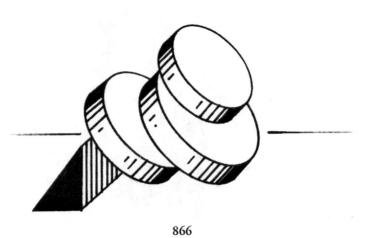

866

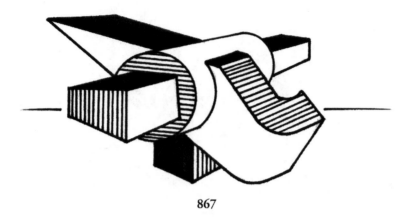

867

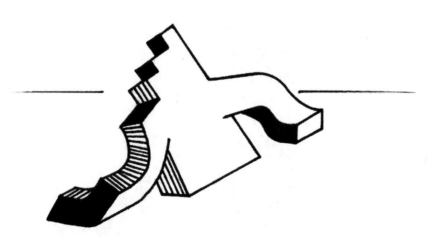

868

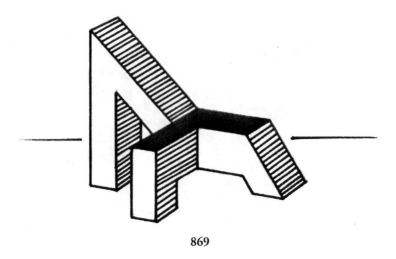

869

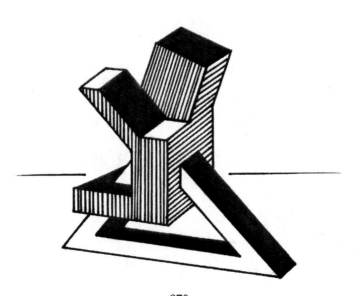

870

871

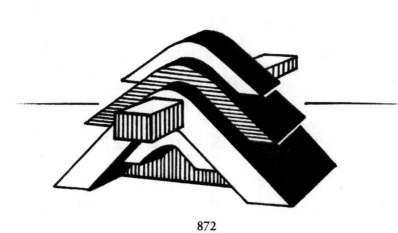

872

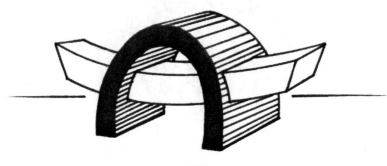

873

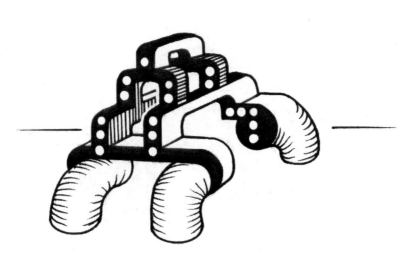

874

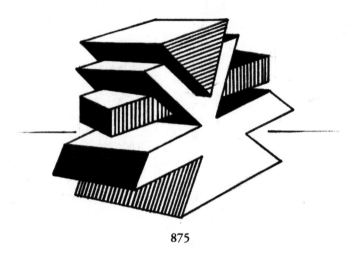

875

876

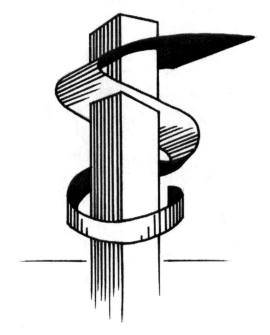

877

878

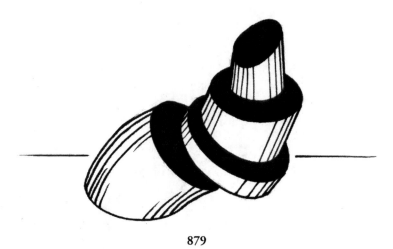

879

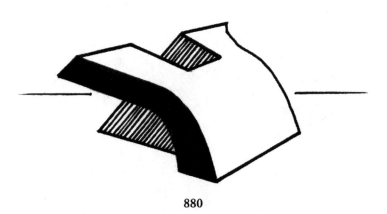

880

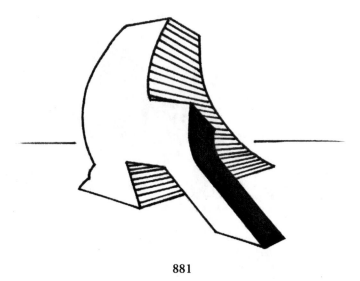

881

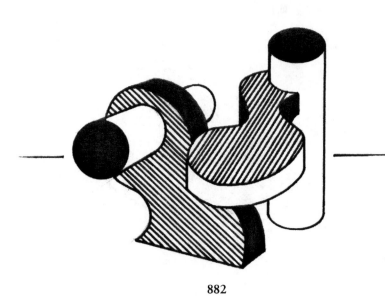

882

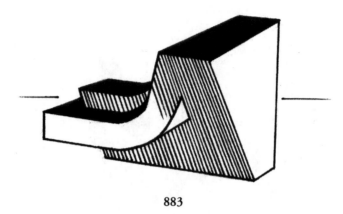

883

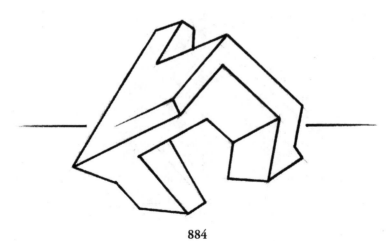

884

885

886

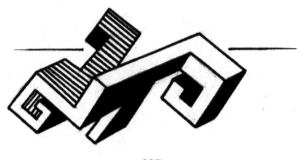

887

888

889

890

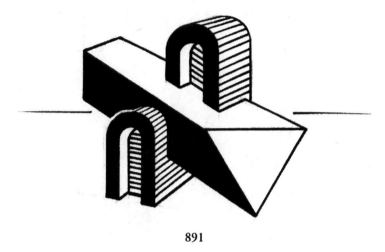

891

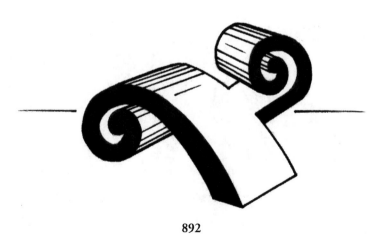

892

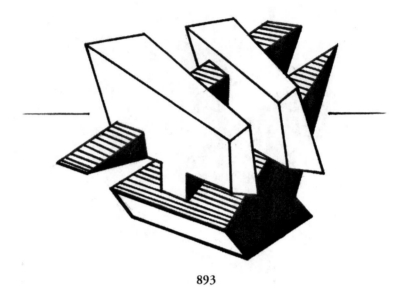

893

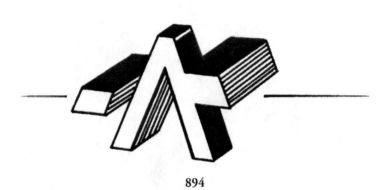

894

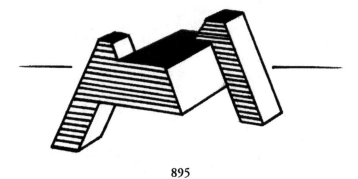

895

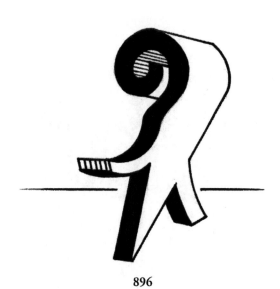

896

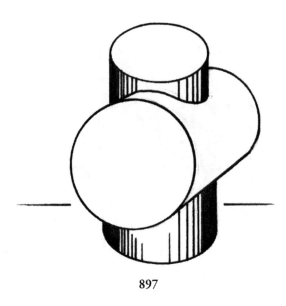

897

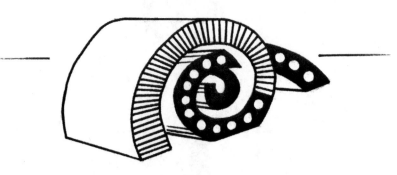

898

899

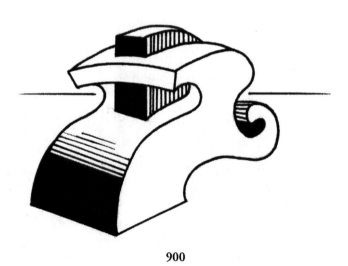

900

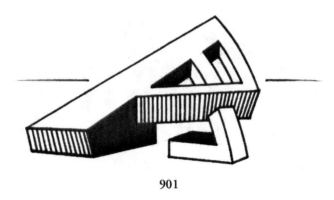

901

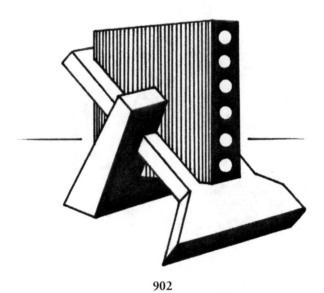

902

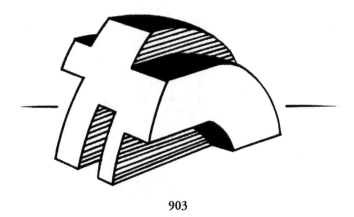

903

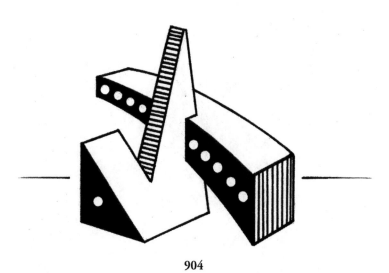

904

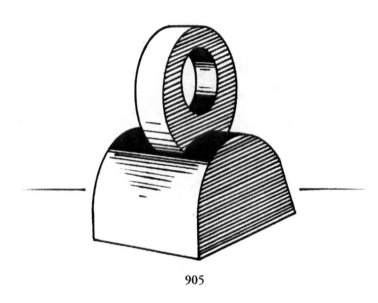

905

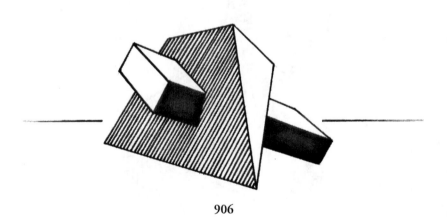

906

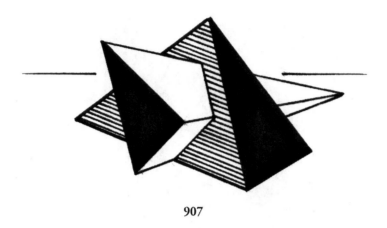

907

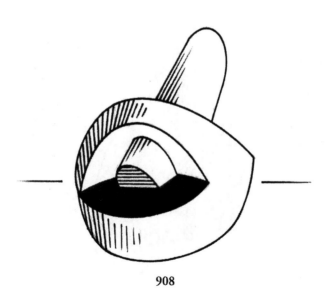

908

909

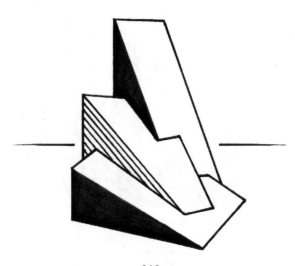

910

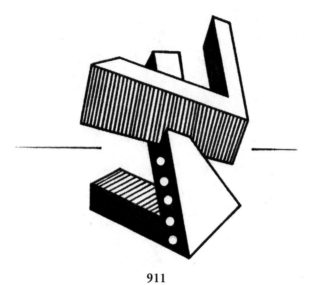

911

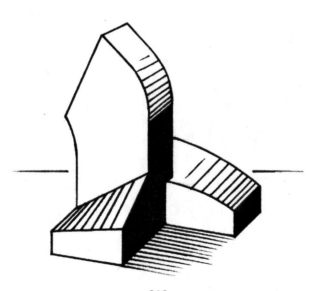

912

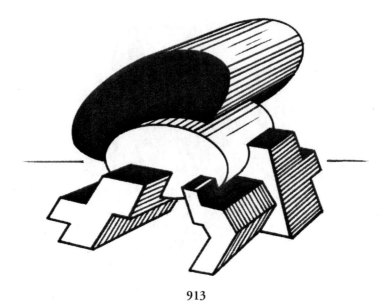

913

914

915

916

917

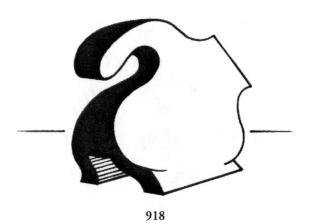

918

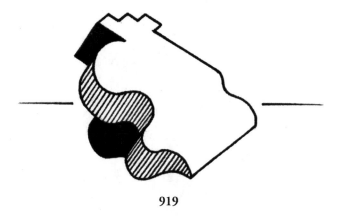

919

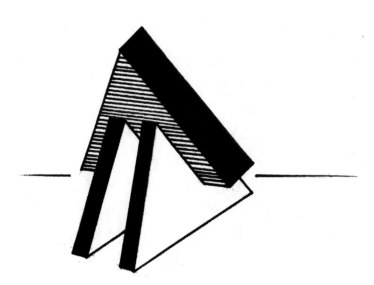

920

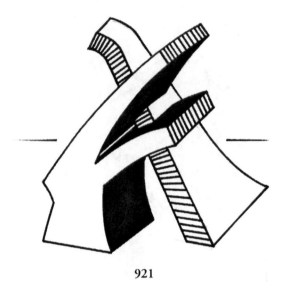

921

922

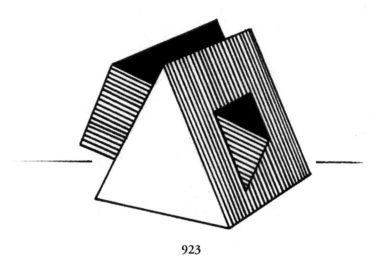

923

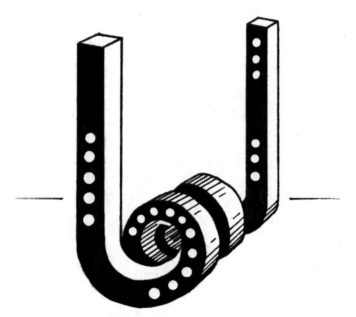

924

925

926

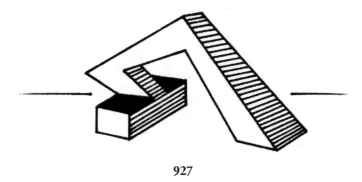

927

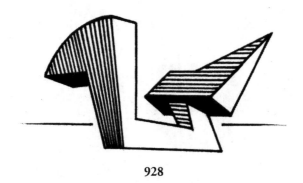

928

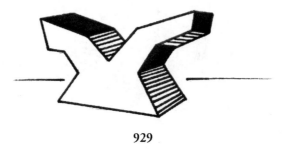

929

930

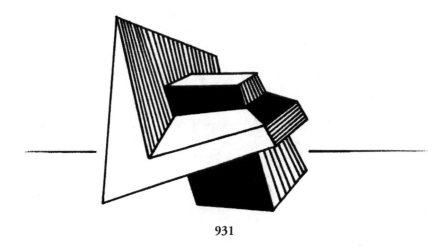

931

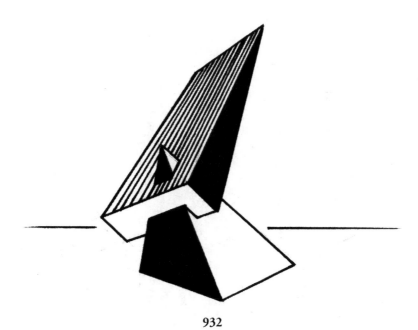

932

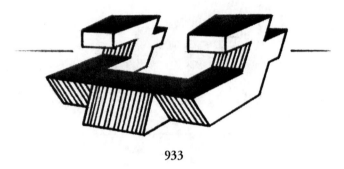

933

934

935

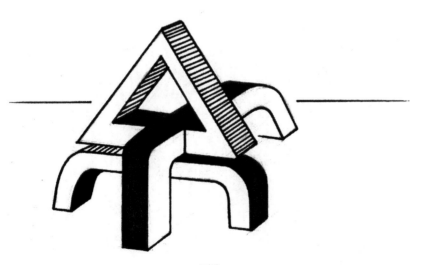

936

937

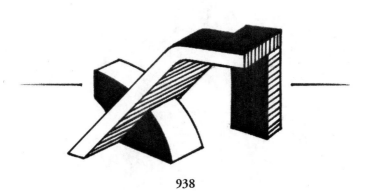

938

939

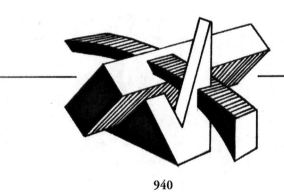

940

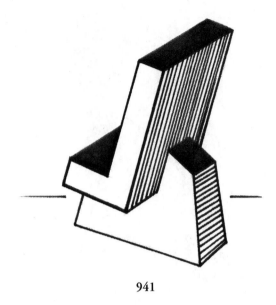

941

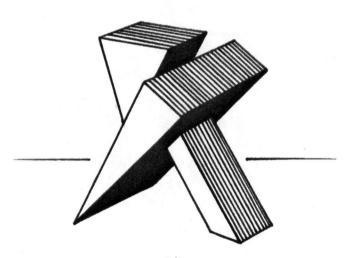

942

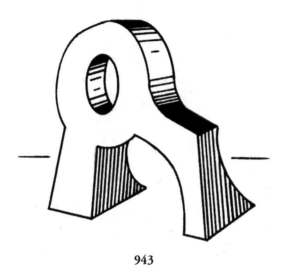

943

944

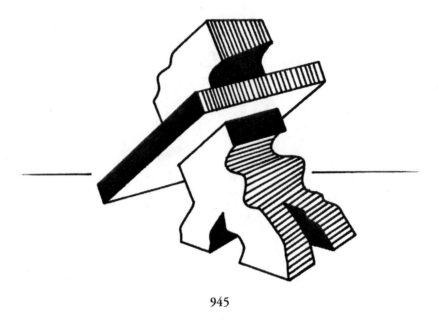

945

946

947

948

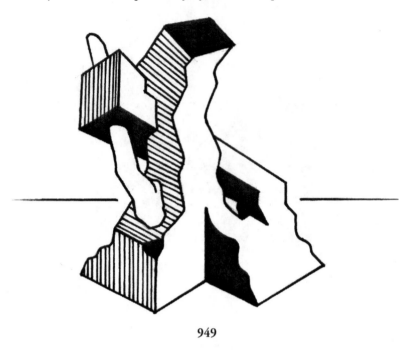

949

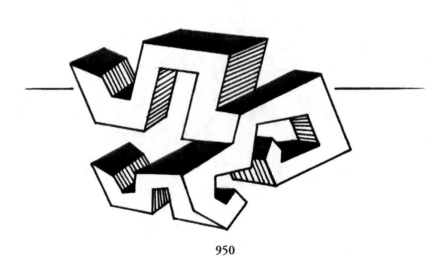

950

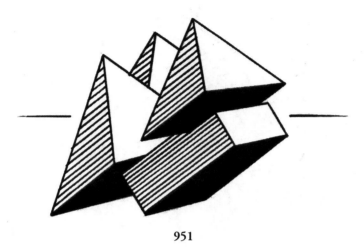

951

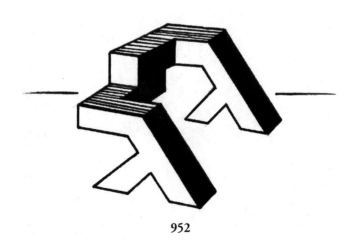

952

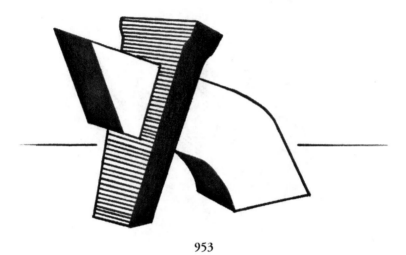

953

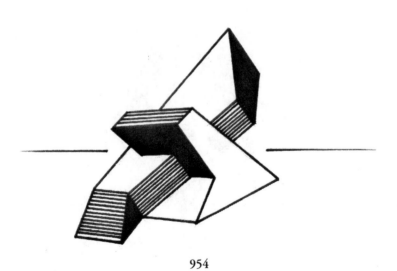

954

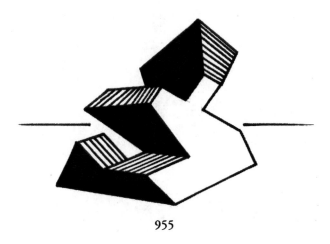

955

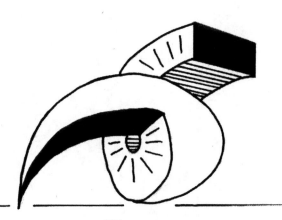

956

957

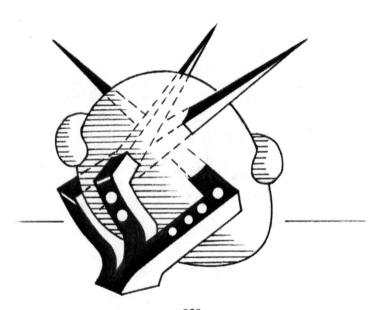

958

959

960

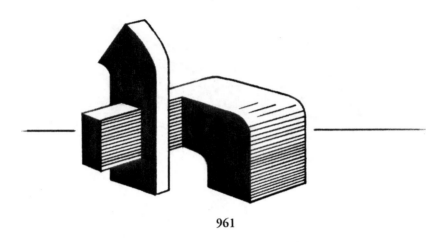

961

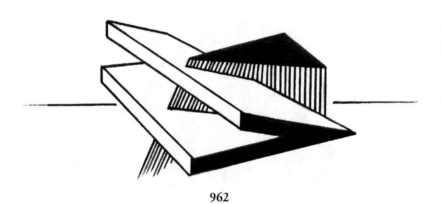

962

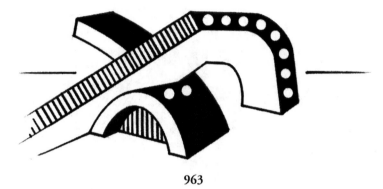

963

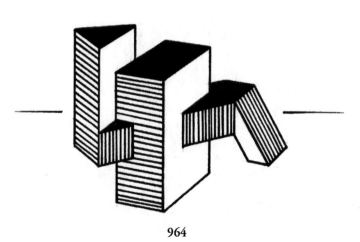

964

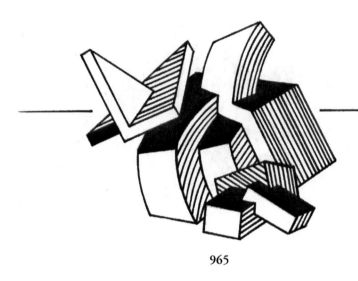

965

966

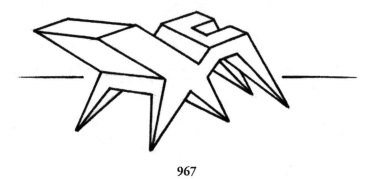

967

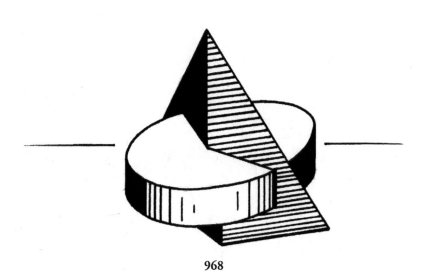

968

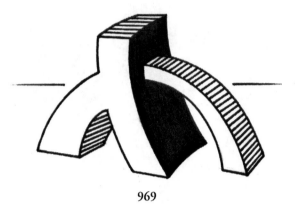

969

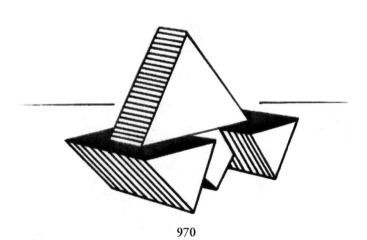

970

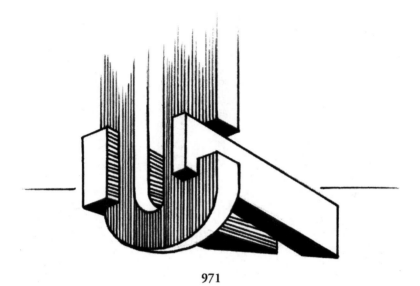

971

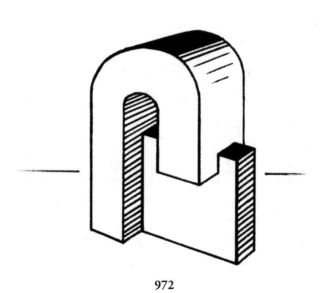

972

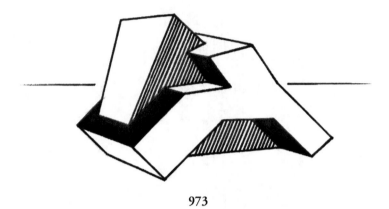

973

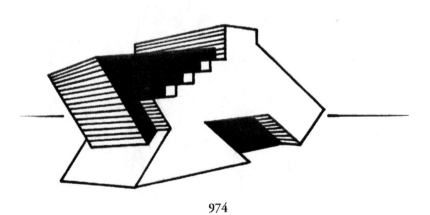

974

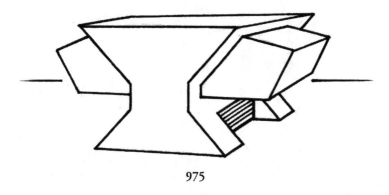

975

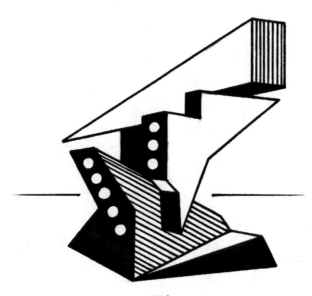

976

977

978

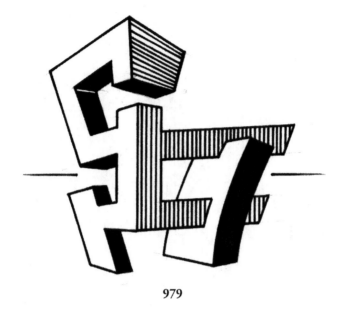

979

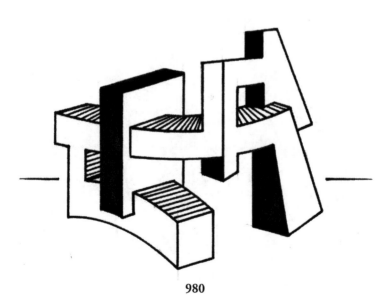

980

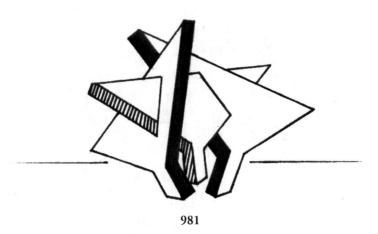

981

982

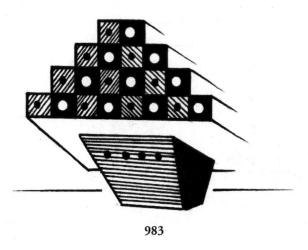

983

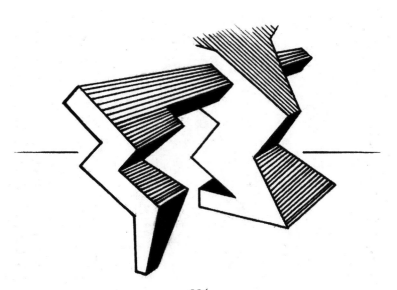

984

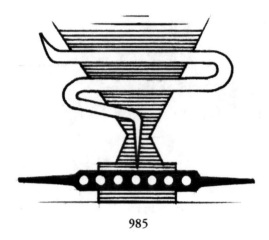

985

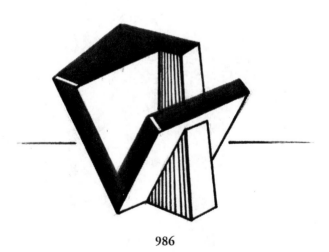

986

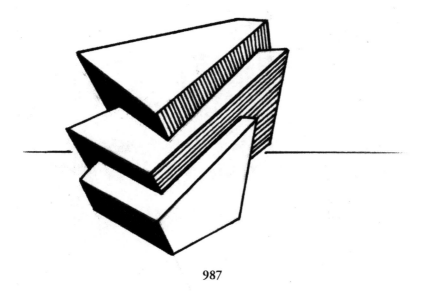

987

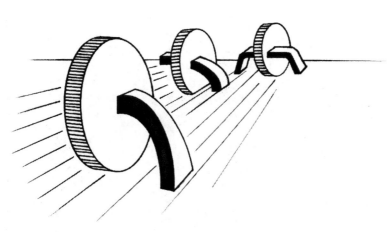

988

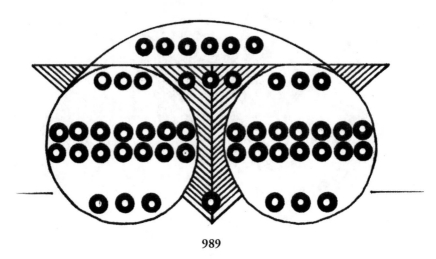

989

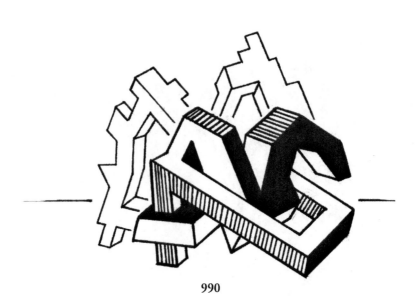

990

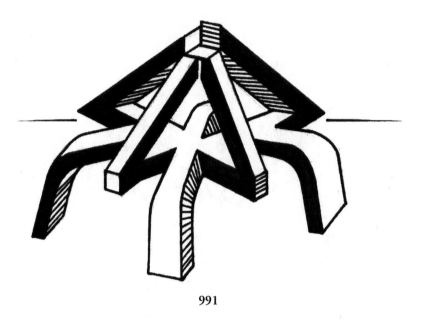

991

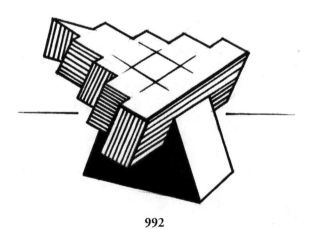

992

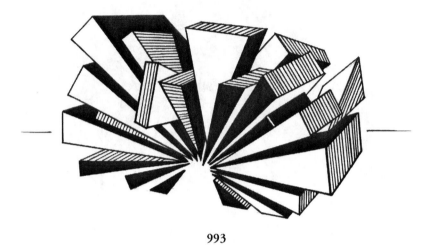

993

994

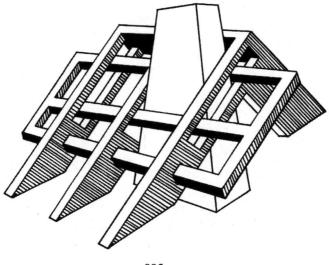

995

996

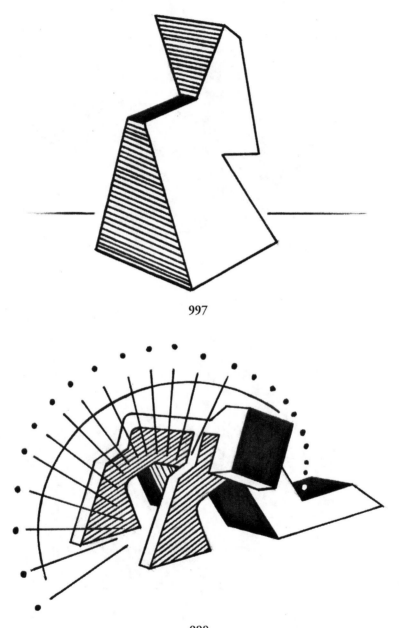

997

998

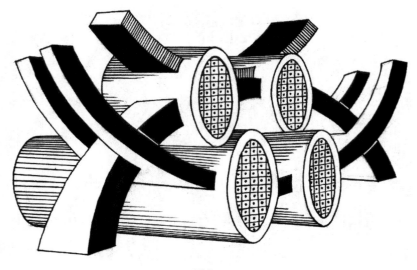

999

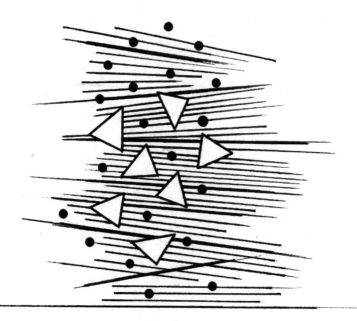

1000

1001